Simple Recipes Using Food Storage

CHOICE ▽ QUALITY

CFI
Springville, Utah

ISBN 13: 978-1-59955-107-4

Published by CFI, an imprint of Cedar Fort, Inc., 2373 W. 700 S., Springville, UT, 84663
Distributed by Cedar Fort, Inc. www.cedarfort.com

LIBRARY OF CONGRESS CATALOGING-IN-PUBLICATION DATA

Simple recipes using food storage.
       p. cm.
Includes index.
ISBN 978-1-59955-107-4
1. Quick and easy cookery. 2. Food—Storage. I. Cedar Fort, Inc. II. Title.

TX833.5.S57 2008
641.5'55—dc22

2007032275

Cover design by Nicole Williams
Cover design © 2008 by Lyle Mortimer
Edited and typeset by Lyndsee Simpson Cordes

Printed in the United States of America

10 9 8 7 6 5 4 3 2 1

Printed on acid-free paper

Table of Contents

Cheat Sheet

Frequently Asked Questions and Handy Tips

Part I

The Basics

"The Lord giveth no commandments unto the children of men, save he shall prepare a way for them that they may accomplish the thing which he commandeth them."

· 1 Nephi 3:7

Using whole wheat flour

• Use wheat in recipes your family already likes, so it is not totally unfamiliar and you know your family will eat it.

• Try wheat in desserts first—who can turn down a cookie?

• Don't feel you have to use 100% whole wheat flour. Half white and half wheat gives excellent results.

• When substituting whole wheat flour for white in your favorite recipes, remember:

1. Wheat flour is heavier than white flour and needs more leavening.

2. In yeast breads, use more yeast and let it rise longer.

3. In recipes that use baking powder for leavening, increase baking powder by 1 tsp. for each 3 cups of whole wheat flour.

4. Recipes using baking soda do not need to be adjusted.

Using wheat

• Buy good wheat (hard wheat is best) that is low in moisture (less than 10%) and clean. Be sure to check for insects.

• Store in containers with tight lids (canned is best).

• If not canned, check every few months for insect infestation.

• Whole wheat flour may be used in place of white flour, measure for measure.

• For light whole wheat flour, used in place of white flour, combine ¾ cup whole wheat flour with ¼ cup cornstarch for every cup of white flour.

• As an excellent meat extender, bring 1 cup water to a boil and cook ⅓ cup cracked wheat, salt, and a beef bouillon cube. Simmer well for best results. This equals 1 lb. of meat. (This works especially well in meat loaf.)

- Grind only the amount of wheat flour needed, or place ground flour in tightly covered container and store in the freezer to minimize loss of nutrients. Most of the essential vitamins oxidize within 72 hours if precautions are not taken.
- Run wheat through a grinder several times for a lighter flour.
- If using 1 cup honey to replace 1 cup sugar, reduce other liquids in recipe by ¼ cup for each cup of honey used.
- Use your imagination! Wheat can be used to make just about anything.

Using sweeteners

- White granulated sugar, if stored in a cool, dry place in a sealed container, will usually store indefinitely.
- Brown sugar should be kept in containers with tight fitting lids to keep the original moisture in.
- Powdered sugar should also be kept in a dry container with a tight fitting lid.
- You can make powdered sugar by blending granulated sugar on high.
- If corn syrup crystallizes after long storage, place container in a pan of hot water to melt the crystals. It stores well in a sealed container placed in a cool, dark, dry location.
- Fructose is ⅓ sweeter than sugar, so if a recipe calls for 1 cup sugar, you can use ⅔ cup of fructose.
- Other products in the sugar category that you may wish to store include jams, jellies, and preserves; flavored gelatins and puddings; powdered drink mixes; sweet toppings; syrups (maple, corn, etc.); molasses; hard candy and gum; and soft drinks.

Using honey

• Honey, if properly refined and stored at room temperature in a cool, dry place, will keep indefinitely. It will darken with age and heat. Age can also cause honey to crystallize. This does not harm it. It can be reliquefied by placing the bottle in a pan of hot water until the crystals disappear. Do not boil.

• Store honey in containers with tight fitting lids. When left uncovered, honey picks up other odors and loses its own aroma. Uncovered, it will also absorb unwanted moisture, which could alter the texture, taste, and storage life.

• Honey is sweeter than sugar. If a recipe calls for 1 cup sugar, you can use ¾ cup honey. Except in the following, honey may be used measure for measure in place of sugar: baked apples, baked ham, candied vegetables, custards, dressing for salads, glazes, lemonade, pie fillings, puddings, and sweet and sour dishes.

• When baking with honey as a substitute for sugar, reduce the other liquid in the recipe by ¼ cup for every cup of sugar substituted. (For example, 1 cup sugar = ¾ cup honey minus ¼ cup liquid.)

• Honey is acidic. In baked goods, add ¼ tsp. baking soda per cup of sugar substituted.

• Bake at 25 degrees lower temperature than original recipe when using honey.

• Make it a rule to combine honey with the liquid ingredients first to assure complete distribution in the mixture.

• To measure honey with ease, wet or spray your measuring utensils first, or measure oil first and use the same cup for honey.

• Brown sugar can be made from honey mixed with molasses. Add 2 Tbsp. of molasses to every ½ cup of honey.

Part 2

Step by Step

"We can begin with a one week's food supply and gradually build it to a month, and then to three months."[1]

• *President Gordon B. Hinckley*

Step 1

For recipes in this section, you will need:
  Wheat
  Oil
  Salt
  Honey or sugar
  Water

Wheat Berries
• •

1 cup clean, whole wheat kernels
5 cups water

Combine wheat and water. Bring to a boil in covered pot. Boil 2 minutes and remove from heat. Let stand 1 hour. • Bring to a boil for the second time. Simmer until tender, about 30 minutes. • Drain, saving liquid for use in gravies and sauces.

Makes about 4 cups.

 ## How do I use Wheat Berries?

Wheat berries can be used in a variety of ways. They are used in various forms (whole, cracked, bulgur, or sprouted) for different end products and textures. Cooked wheat can be stored in the refrigerator or frozen for later use.

Whole Wheat Cereal

Slow Cooker Method:
1 cup whole wheat kernels
2½ cups water
½ tsp. salt

Combine all ingredients in a slow cooker and cook 6–8 hours or overnight on low. • Add milk and sweetener for a tasty hot cereal.

Thermos Method:
1 cup whole wheat kernels
2 cups boiling water
½ tsp. salt

Combine all ingredients in a quart-sized thermos; screw top lightly. Leave overnight. • In the morning you'll have tasty, hot cereal, ready to eat.

Whole Wheat Flour Tortillas

2 cups wheat or white flour
½–¾ cup water
1 tsp. salt
2 Tbsp. oil

Mix ingredients together and knead well. Add small amount of water, if necessary. Let stand for 10 minutes. • Knead and pat or slap into the shape of a thin pancake. Add more water or flour as needed. • Cook on top of the stove in ungreased, heavy iron or non-stick skillet, turning to cook through, but do not burn.

Wheat Treats

1½ cups wheat kernels
cold water
oil for deep frying
honey glaze (recipe below), or desired seasonings, such as garlic,
   celery, onion, or seasoned salts (optional)

Soak wheat in cold water for 24 hours, changing water once or twice during this period, or boil wheat for 30 minutes. Wheat will triple in volume. • Drain wheat and rinse. Remove excess water by rolling wheat on a cloth or paper towel. • In a heavy kettle, heat vegetable oil to 360 degrees. Put small amount of wheat (about 1½ cups) in a wire basket or strainer and deep fry in hot oil for 90 seconds. • Drain on absorbent paper.

Honey Glaze:
1 Tbsp. water
1 cup honey

Boil to a hard-crack stage (300–310 degrees). Drop a spoonful of hot mixture into a bowl of very cold water. If the syrup forms brittle threads in the water and cracks if you try to mold it, it is ready. • Pour over Wheat Treats.

Wheat Flakes

2 cups coarsely ground whole wheat flour
2 cups water
1 tsp. salt

Mix all ingredients lightly with spoon until free of lumps. Beat just until mixed. Pour into cookie sheet or jelly roll pan. Use ½ cup dough on a 12x15-inch cookie sheet. Tip sheet back and forth to cover entire surface. Drain excess (about ¼ cup) from one corner, leaving a thin film. • Bake at 350 degrees for 15 minutes. • Break into bite-sized pieces.

Sprouted Wheat

1 cup raw wheat kernels
1 gallon-sized, wide-mouth glass jar
4 cups warm water
cheesecloth or nylon net
large rubber band

Day 1: Sort wheat kernels, removing damaged ones. Rinse in cool water to clean. • Put kernels in jar; add warm water. Cover jar with several layers of cheesecloth or nylon net. Secure with rubber band. • Soak for 8 hours or overnight.

Day 2: Drain off water. Water contains some nutrients and may be added to soups or used to water houseplants. Lay the jar on its side in a warm, dark place. • Rinse kernels in cool water 2–3 times a day. This prevents spoiling or souring.

Day 3 (and on): Rinse sprouts in cool water several times a day until they reach the desired growth. Sprouts should be about ¼ inch long for use in baked goods. • Longer sprouts may cause a soggy product. Longer sprouts may be used when raw sprouts are called for. • When sprouts reach desired length, refrigerate them and plan to use within several days.

 Using sprouted wheat

• Serve raw in salads.
• Steam lightly and serve as a vegetable, either alone or in combination with other vegetables.
• Add to soups, stews, casseroles, or egg dishes, usually just before serving.
• Chop or use whole in baked goods or sandwiches.
• Liquefy in blender and add to drinks or soups.

What is cracked wheat?

Cracked wheat is a wheat berry, broken into small pieces. Nutritionally it is the same as whole wheat, rich in cereal protein, B vitamins, and iron. It differs from bulgur in that bulgur is precooked. To crack wheat into modest-sized pieces, place whole wheat berries in a mill or grinder set on the coarsest setting or in a food processor for a few seconds. It's best to only grind what you will be using. If you choose to grind an extra amount, place it in a sealed container and store in the freezer.

Basic Cooked Cracked Wheat

3 cups liquid (water, fruit juice, broth)
I cup cracked wheat
I tsp. salt

Combine ingredients and bring to a boil. Cover, reduce heat, and simmer 20–30 minutes or until tender. • Note: Use fruit juice to cook the wheat if it is to be used in fruit salad; water or broth for main dishes, bread, or cereal.

Makes about 2½ cups cooked cracked wheat.

Basic Hot Cracked Wheat Cereal

I cup cracked wheat
2½ cups water
½ tsp. salt

Combine and bring to a boil. Cook covered on low for 10–20 minutes. • Add milk and sweetener for a tasty, hot breakfast.

What is bulgur?

Bulgur is usually made from hard red wheat, although soft white wheat can also be used. It can be used in a number of different ways and can replace rice in most recipes. The volume doubles, approximately, when it is cooked or soaked. Since it is precooked, bulgur keeps longer and cooks faster than cracked wheat kernels, and it has a slightly different flavor. This flavor can be best described as nutty and is enhanced by browning bulgur in a bit of oil before cooking. Bulgur can be eaten as cereal, used as a meat extender, or added to breads, salads, and casseroles. Cooked bulgur freezes.

Homemade Bulgur

1 cup wheat berries, cleaned
2 cups water

Rinse wheat in cool water and then discard water. Combine wheat and 2 cups water and bring to a boil. Cover and simmer 1 hour. Drain off any liquid to use in soups or gravies. • Spread wheat thinly on cookie sheet or shallow pan and dry in oven at 200 degrees until very dry (about 2 hours). When it cracks easily, it's done. Leave oven door open a crack so moisture can escape. • Crack wheat into moderate pieces using a mill or grinder. In some cases the wheat may be used whole, giving a very chewy product. • This processed bulgur, when thoroughly dried, is easily stored (in a cool, dry place) and may be used in many wheat recipes. • If the recipe calls for cooked wheat or bulgur, simply boil in water 5–10 minutes; it will approximately double in volume.

Basic Bulgur

1 cup bulgur
2 cups water
½ tsp. salt

Combine ingredients in saucepan. • Cover and bring to boil. • Reduce heat and simmer about 15 minutes.

Makes about 2½ cups cooked bulgur.

Wheat Thins

3¼ cups whole wheat flour (or equal parts whole wheat flour and white flour)
⅓ cup oil
¾ tsp. salt or onion salt
1 cup water

Mix flours together in medium bowl. • In blender, mix oil, salt, and water; add this to flour mixture. • Knead as little as possible to make a smooth dough. • Roll dough as thin as possible on ungreased cookie sheet (not more than ⅛-inch thick). • Mark with knife to size of crackers desired, but do not cut through. • Prick each cracker a few times with a fork. • Sprinkle dough lightly with salt or onion salt as desired. • Bake at 350 degrees until crisp and light brown, 30–35 minutes. • Break crackers apart along knife marks.

? What is gluten?

Raw gluten can be made into flour or used as a meat substitute. Making gluten at home can be a lot of work. If you wish to make your own gluten from hard red wheat, first grind it into flour. Or you may start with purchased whole wheat flour. Hard wheat varieties usually have more protein and therefore have more gluten content than soft wheat.

Basic Raw Gluten
• •

Gluten is called "Meat from Wheat" because it is often used as a meat substitute. Used in combination with eggs, milk, or cheese, it makes a complete protein package. See Step 2 of this section for more recipes using gluten as a meat substitute.

9 cups cold water
18 cups whole wheat flour

Place water in a large bowl. Add 6 cups of flour, beating well. Add another 6 cups flour and beat until dough is very elastic. Add the last 6 cups slowly as the mixture gets very stiff. If you have a heavy-duty mixer with a dough hook, use it to develop the gluten into a very elastic mass. If not, turn the dough out onto a floured board and knead roughly. • The gluten is well developed when the dough gets hard to knead and bounces back when pushed down. It should also be very smooth.

Put the dough back into the bowl and cover with cold water. Let sit for at least 2 hours or overnight. • Pour off the excess water. This drained liquid contains starch, bran, and some nutrients, so save it for use in soups, gravies, or as liquid in bread making. • Continue kneading and rinsing the gluten until the water poured off is clear. What remains is raw gluten. It is a tough, sticky, somewhat elastic substance that has almost no taste.

Gluten Flour

. . . .

Use in recipes calling for gluten flour. You may also substitute it for equal amounts of flour in bread recipes. Use no more than 1 cup gluten flour per 4-loaf recipes with this homemade gluten.

Spread out raw gluten (pg. 16) about ½-inch thick on a lightly oiled baking sheet. • Bake 15 minutes at 350 degrees. Break any bubbles to let steam out. • Bake another 15 minutes or until it springs back when pressed. Cool and grate on largest holes of a shredder. It will be soft and pliable. • Spread on a baking sheet; bake at 200 degrees until it is completely dry. Grind into flour.

Step 2

Now add:
    Yeast
    Spices and flavorings
    Baking powder
    Powdered milk
    Powdered eggs
    Vinegar
    Baking soda
    Lemon juice

Types of powdered milk

1. **Instant** (nonfat): Mixes easily with water, great for hot chocolate mixes, less concentrated than non-instant, but more expensive than non-instant.

2. **Non-instant** (also nonfat): Requires vigorous hand mixing or electric blender or mixer to disperse with the water, mixes best when water is warm, more concentrated than instant. Morning Moo and other whey-based products are good to drink, but they do not work in the following recipes.

• *In the following recipes, use either powdered milk or regular milk. If using powdered milk, either reconstitute before adding or mix powder with the dry ingredients and the corresponding water with the wet ingredients.*

Storing powdered milk

• Powdered milk can be stored in air-tight containers at room temperature for two years before it begins to stale. At cooler temperatures, it can last longer.

• In the 1979 Essentials of Home Production and Storage pamphlet, the Church recommends that members store an equivalent of 300 quarts of powdered milk, or approximately 75 lbs. of powdered milk per person per year.

• As milk ages, its flavor changes. Even past its prime, milk still has some nutritional value and is still safe to use. If milk has been contaminated or spoiled due to insects, rodents, or moisture, discard immediately.

• Milk that is too old to drink can be used in cooking as long as it hasn't spoiled or been contaminated.

• Spoiled powdered milk can be used as fertilizer.

• Foods made with powdered milk will have fewer calories and less cholesterol than those made from whole milk. Adding additional milk to the recipe will enhance the nutritive value of the recipe.[2]

Reconstituted Milk . . . .

1 cup water
⅓ cup powdered milk

Blend thoroughly.

Evaporated Milk . . . .

1 cup water
⅔ cup powdered milk

Blend thoroughly.

Can I substitute powdered milk for regular?

In any recipe calling for milk, simply add the powdered milk to the other dry ingredients. Sift to blend, then add water for the milk called for in the recipe.

Whipped Evaporated Milk

1 cup evaporated milk (pg. 19)
2 Tbsp. lemon juice

Thoroughly chill evaporated milk. Add lemon juice and whip until stiff. Sweeten and flavor as desired.

Makes 3 cups.

Sweetened Condensed Milk

½ cup hot water
1 cup powdered milk
1 cup sugar

Blend thoroughly in blender. Can be stored in refrigerator or frozen.

Buttermilk or Sour Milk

1 cup water
1 Tbsp. vinegar or lemon juice
⅓ cup powdered milk

Can I drink powdered milk?

Powdered milk tastes similar to regular milk. To improve the flavor of powdered milk, mix it half and half with whole or 2% milk. You may try adding a little sugar or vanilla to enhance the flavor. Let it chill for several hours before drinking.

Everlasting Yeast

. . . .

By keeping the everlasting yeast start and remaking some each time, yeast can be kept indefinitely.

1 quart warm potato water*
½ yeast cake or ½ Tbsp. dry yeast
1 tsp. salt
2 Tbsp. sugar
2 cups white or whole wheat flour

Stir all ingredients together. Place mixture in warm place to rise until ready to use for baking. Leave a small amount (about ¾–1 cup) of everlasting yeast for a start for next time. • Between uses, keep in covered jar in refrigerator until a few hours before ready to use again. • Add same ingredients, except yeast, to the everlasting yeast start for the next baking.

*For potato water, strain excess water after boiling potatoes, refrigerate in airtight container.

Baking with eggs

In baked products using eggs, separate the eggs and beat the whites until stiff. Then fold in just before baking. For extra lightness, an extra separated egg may be added; this works especially well for waffles and cakes.

Baking Powder Biscuits

2 cups whole wheat or white flour
3 tsp. baking powder
½ tsp. salt
4 Tbsp. oil
⅔–¾ cup milk

Sift flour with salt and baking powder. Add oil, and mix until crumbly. Add milk, and mix just until milk is incorporated. • Turn out on lightly floured surface; knead gently 30 seconds. Roll or pat ½-inch thick and cut out biscuits with a biscuit cutter, an empty tuna can, or a glass. • Bake on ungreased cookie sheet at 450 degrees for 12–15 minutes.

Makes 6–8 medium sized biscuits.

Whole Wheat Muffins

2 cups whole wheat or white flour
¼ cup sugar
½ tsp. salt
3 tsp. baking powder
¼ cup oil
1 egg
1 cup milk (or ⅓ cup powdered milk and 1 cup water)

Mix all dry ingredients together in a medium bowl. If you are using powdered milk, mix powdered milk with dry ingredients. • In large measuring cup, combine liquid ingredients. Pour over dry ingredients and stir just until moistened. • Spoon into greased muffin tins and bake at 425 degrees for 18–20 minutes or until golden brown.

Makes 12 muffins.

Whole Wheat Bread
. . . .

2 pkgs. (2 Tbsp.) dry yeast
⅓ cup honey
3½ cups warm water (120 degrees)
1 Tbsp. salt
⅓ cup oil
7 cups whole wheat flour (approximately)

Place warm water, yeast, and honey in heavy-duty mixer. Mix on low for a few seconds. When the yeast has activated (bubbles will appear) add the oil and salt. Mix briefly. • Then add about half of the flour. Knead. Slowly add rest of flour until dough just pulls away from the side of the mixing bowl (dough will be a little sticky). This normally will take most of the whole wheat flour. Adding too little flour is generally better than adding too much. • Allow your mixer to knead the dough until the gluten in the whole wheat flour is properly developed. This will take anywhere from 12–18 minutes, depending on the strength and durability of your mixer.

After this kneading, cover the dough and let it rest in the bowl and rise until doubled. Punch down. At this point you may let it rise again or, with oiled hands, remove the dough from the bowl (the dough should be elastic with a silky appearance and should stick to itself instead of to you or the bowl). • Shape dough into loaves. (Yield: 3 loaves in 4½x8½-inch pans or 4–5 loaves in 3x5¾-inch pans) and place in well-greased pans. Let loaves rise in a warm place until doubled (a slightly warmed oven works well—no hotter than 85 degrees). • Bake at 350 degrees for 30–45 minutes, depending on the size of the loaf. If loaves have been rising in warm oven, just turn temperature up when ready to bake. The rise will be enhanced as the oven heats up to baking temperature. • When loaves are done, immediately remove from pans and let cool on wire rack. (Wipe out pans while hot and you won't have to wash them).

Sweet Muffins

1½ cups flour
½ cup sugar
½ tsp. salt
2 tsp. baking powder
¼ cup oil
1 egg
½ cup milk
dried fruit or drained, canned fruit (optional)

Mix all dry ingredients together in a medium bowl. If using powdered milk, mix with dry ingredients. • In large measuring cup, combine liquid ingredients (and fruit, if desired). Pour over dry ingredients and stir just until moistened. • Spoon into greased muffin tins and bake at 425 degrees for 18–20 minutes or until golden brown.

Makes 12 muffins.

Wheat Nuts

3 cups coarse ground flour
2 tsp. baking powder
½ tsp. salt
1 cup sugar
1 cup milk

Combine all ingredients. Dough will be sticky. • Pour ½-inch thick onto greased baking sheet. Bake at 350 degrees for 30–35 minutes till firm but not crisp. • Cut cereal into chunks. Turn them upside down and return to the warm oven until dried out thoroughly. • Grind in meat grinder with coarse disk or pound with meat mallet.

Indian Fry Bread

2 cups wheat or white flour
2 Tbsp. oil
½ cup powdered milk
I Tbsp. baking powder
¾ cup lukewarm water
¾ tsp. salt

In mixing bowl, combine flour, powdered milk, baking powder, and salt. Add oil and warm water. • Knead dough until smooth. If dough is too tough, add more warm water. Dough should be elastic but not sticky. Allow to stand 30 minutes or overnight. • Pat into 2-inch thick patties. Heat about 1 cup oil in skillet on medium heat. Drop patties into oil and cook until golden brown, about 1 minute on each side. • Drain on paper towel and serve with honey or honey butter.

Crunchy Wheat Cereal

6 cups whole wheat flour
I tsp. baking soda
½ tsp. salt
1½ cups sugar or brown sugar
2 cups buttermilk or milk, or ⅔ cup powdered milk, 2 cups water, and 2 Tbsp. vinegar or lemon juice

Mix ingredients thoroughly. Press or roll evenly to fit two ungreased cookie sheets. • Bake at 350 degrees until golden brown around edges. Turn over with spatula, break into small pieces, and return to 200-degree oven to dry out thoroughly. • Grind chunks in food or meat chopper on coarse blade. Put ground chunks in strainer and sift out small granular pieces. Larger pieces may be used for cereal and casseroles. Finer pieces may be used as graham cracker crumbs for pie crusts and other desserts.

Makes approximately 5 cups cereal and 2 cups crumbs.

Blender Mayonnaise

1 egg, unbeaten
1 cup oil
¾ tsp. salt

Place egg and salt in blender. Add ¼ cup of the oil. • Blend on low speed while adding the remaining oil gradually in a steady stream. Stop occasionally to push oil into mayonnaise.

Variations
• For different flavors, add ½ tsp. dry mustard, ¼ tsp. paprika, 1 Tbsp. lemon juice, or 1 Tbsp. vinegar.

Basic Pasta

2⅓ cups whole wheat or white flour, divided
2 beaten eggs
½ tsp. salt
1 tsp. oil
⅓ cup water

In large mixing bowl, stir together 2 cups of flour and salt. Push the mixture against the edge of the bowl, making a well in the center. • In a small bowl, combine eggs, water, and oil. Pour egg mixture into the well of the flour mixture all at once and stir until the dry and liquid ingredients are well combined. • Sprinkle the kneading surface with the remaining ⅓ cup flour. Turn dough out onto the floured surface. Knead till dough is smooth and elastic, about 8–10 minutes. Cover and let rest 10 minutes.

Divide dough into thirds or fourths. On a lightly floured surface, roll each third piece of dough into a 16x12-inch rectangle or each fourth of dough into a 12-inch square. If using a pasta machine, pass dough through the machine till ¹⁄₁₆-inch thick. • Dust with additional flour, as necessary, to prevent sticking. Cut and shape as desired (use your imagination: spirals, corkscrews, bowties, etc.).
Makes 1 lb. of fresh pasta, about 4 cups cooked pasta.

Whole Wheat Pasta

1 beaten egg
2 Tbsp. milk
½ tsp. salt
1 cup whole wheat or white flour

In mixing bowl, combine egg, milk, and salt. Stir in enough flour to make stiff dough. Cover and let rest for 10 minutes. • On a floured surface, roll dough into 16x12-inch rectangle. Let stand 10 minutes. • Roll up loosely; cut into ¼-inch thick slices. Unroll and cut noodles into desired lengths. Spread out and let dry on rack 2 hours. Store in airtight container till ready to use. • Drop noodles into a large amount of boiling water or soup. Cook uncovered 10–12 minutes or until done.

Makes about 3 cups.

 How do I cook fresh pasta?

To cook 8 oz. fresh pasta, bring 3 qt. salted water to boil. Add 1 Tbsp. oil to water to keep large pasta separated. When water is boiling vigorously, add pasta a little at a time so water does not stop boiling. • Reduce heat slightly and continue boiling, uncovered, until pasta is tender but still slightly firm. Stir occasionally to prevent pasta from sticking. Taste often near the end of cooking time to test for doneness. • When done, immediately drain in colander. Transfer to warm serving dish and serve immediately.

Blender Wheat Pancakes

1 cup milk or ⅓ cup nonfat powdered milk and 1 cup water
1 cup uncooked whole wheat kernels
2 eggs
2 tsp. baking powder
2 Tbsp. oil
2 Tbsp. honey or sugar
½ tsp. salt

Combine milk and wheat in blender. Blend on highest speed for 4–5 minutes or until batter is smooth. • Add eggs, oil, baking powder, honey, and salt. Blend on low. Cook on hot griddle.

Makes 6–8 pancakes.

Variations:
• Pancakes: Add 1 unpeeled, cored apple and 1 tsp. cinnamon to blender. Serve with applesauce and whipped topping.
• Waffles: Add 1 additional Tbsp. wheat and increase oil to 4 Tbsp.

Wheat Waffles

2 cups whole wheat or white flour
2 eggs
4 tsp. baking powder
½ tsp. salt
2 Tbsp. honey or sugar
6 Tbsp. oil
1¾ cups milk or ⅔ cup nonfat powdered milk and 1¾ cups water

Mix dry ingredients together, including nonfat powdered milk. Stir in remaining ingredients. • For lighter waffles, separate eggs, beat egg whites, and carefully fold into mixture.

Makes 8 waffles.

Deluxe Pancakes

3 cups whole wheat flour
1 Tbsp. baking powder
¼ tsp. salt
3 Tbsp. honey
2 eggs, separated
1½ cups milk
3 Tbsp. oil

Combine all ingredients except egg whites. • Beat whites until fluffy and fold into mixture. • Cook on hot griddle.

Swedish Pancakes (Crepes)

2 cups whole wheat wheat or half white and half wheat flour
6 eggs
2 cups milk
4 Tbsp. sugar
¼ tsp. salt
⅔ cup oil
fruit, fresh or frozen (optional)
whipped cream (optional)

Mix eggs and milk. Add flour, sugar, and salt. Blend in oil. • Pour mixture thinly onto oiled hot skillet. Tip to cover bottom of skillet. Flip once and then remove from skillet. • Fill with fresh or frozen fruit. Roll up. Top with whipped cream.

 Using half-and-half flour

• In breads that call for whole wheat flour, you can use half whole wheat flour and half white flour for a lighter bread. Also try buttering the tops of the loaves lightly after taking out of the oven (it makes the crust softer).

German Pancakes

4 eggs
½ tsp. salt
⅔ cup whole wheat or white flour
⅔ cup milk
1 Tbsp. sugar
2 Tbsp. oil

Beat eggs until light in color. Add the rest of the ingredients and mix until smooth. • Pour into 2 well-oiled or buttered 9-inch pans or a 9x13-inch pan. • Bake 10 minutes at 400 degrees and then reduce the heat to 350 degrees and bake another 20 minutes. • These are good topped with melted butter and maple syrup or powdered sugar and lemon juice.

Basic Maple Syrup

4 cups sugar
½ cup brown or white sugar
2 cups water
1 tsp. maple flavoring
1 tsp. vanilla flavoring

In saucepan, mix sugars and water until sugars dissolve. Bring to a boil. Cover and boil gently for 10 minutes. Remove from heat and cool slightly. • Add vanilla and maple flavorings.

Basic Drop Cookies

1¼ cups whole wheat or white flour
½ tsp. baking soda
½ tsp. salt
¼ cup oil
½ cup sugar
¼ cup brown sugar
2 tsp. water
1 egg
1 tsp. vanilla
chocolate chips or nuts (optional)

Combine oil, water, and sugars and mix until smooth. Add the rest of the ingredients and mix well. • Drop by spoonfuls onto a lightly greased cookie sheet. Bake at 350 degrees for 8–10 minutes.

Basic Cake

2 cups whole wheat or white flour
1 Tbsp. baking powder
1 tsp. salt
½ cup oil
1½ cups sugar
1½ tsp. vanilla
1 cup milk
2 eggs

Combine all ingredients and mix well. Pour into greased and floured 9x13-inch baking dish. • Bake at 350 degrees for 30–40 minutes or until done.

Stirred Custard

3 eggs, slightly beaten
2 cups milk
¼ cup sugar
dash of salt
1 tsp. vanilla

In heavy medium-sized saucepan, combine eggs, milk, sugar, and salt. Cook over medium heat while stirring. Continue cooking egg mixture until it coats a metal spoon. • Remove from heat; cool at once by placing pan in a sink or bowl of ice water and stirring 1–2 minutes. Stir in vanilla. • Pour custard mixture into a bowl. Cover surface with clear plastic wrap (unless you like the heavy top coating that forms). • Chill until serving time.

Makes 6 servings.

Vanilla Pudding

½ cup sugar
2 cups milk
¼ cup flour or 2 Tbsp. cornstarch
¼ tsp. salt
1 egg, beaten, or 2 yolks, beaten
1½ tsp. vanilla
2 Tbsp. butter (optional)

In heavy saucepan, combine sugar, flour, and salt. Stir in milk. • Cook and stir over medium heat till thickened and bubbly; cook and stir 2 minutes more. Remove from heat. • Gradually stir about 1 cup of the hot mixture into beaten egg. Return egg mixture to saucepan. • Cook and stir 2 minutes more. Remove from heat. Stir in vanilla (and butter, if desired). Pour into bowl. Cover and chill without stirring.

Step 3
Now add:
  Powdered butter
  Powdered cheese
  Tomatoes

Wheat Muffins
• •

2 cups whole wheat flour
¼ tsp. salt
1 cup white or brown sugar
1 tsp. baking soda
1 cup milk or ⅓ cup powdered milk and 1 cup water
1 egg
½ cup melted margarine
1 tsp. vanilla

Mix dry ingredients in a medium-sized bowl. (If you are using powdered milk, mix powdered milk with dry ingredients.) • In large measuring cup, combine liquid ingredients. Pour over dry ingredients and stir just until moistened. • Spoon into greased muffin tins and bake at 350 degrees for 15 minutes.

Makes 12 muffins.

Pasta & Cheese

I cup uncooked pasta (pg. 26–27)
I Tbsp. powdered butter
2 Tbsp. powdered milk
½ cup water
I Tbsp. powdered cheese

Cook pasta in 4 cups boiling water and 1 tsp. salt. Drain and add other ingredients. • Blend well and heat through.

Makes 4 or 5 servings.

Pizza Dough

2½ cups flour
I Tbsp. yeast
2 Tbsp. oil
2 Tbsp. sugar
I tsp. salt
¾–I cup hot water

Mix together dry ingredients, then add liquid. Knead, adding flour if necessary, until elastic and smooth. • Let sit about 5 minutes, then roll out into crust. • Top with favorite toppings. Bake at 425 degrees for 15–20 minutes.

Makes 1 crust.

Tomato Sauce

Wash and dry fresh, firm tomatoes. Remove core and blossom ends. Cut into quarters. Simmer about 20 minutes, stirring occasionally. • Press through fine sieve or food mill. Cook pulp over medium-high heat until desired thickness. Season as desired for use with pastas and other sauces. • Seal with steam canner or store in fridge to use within 1 week.

Pasta & Cheese Casserole

2 cups uncooked pasta (pg. 26–27)
1 egg, beaten
1 cup dry bread crumbs
2 cups milk
4 Tbsp. reconstituted powdered butter
salt and pepper to taste
½ lb. reconstituted powdered cheese or medium cheddar cheese, shredded

Cook pasta in boiling water until tender. Drain and set aside. • Combine butter and bread crumbs. Stir until well mixed. Set aside. • In separate bowl, beat egg and milk together and add salt and pepper. • In a deep pan or casserole dish, layer ½ of the pasta, cheese, and crumbs. Start again, layering with the rest of the pasta, cheese, and crumbs. • Carefully pour the egg-milk mixture over the top. Add more milk if needed to bring it to the top. • Bake at 350 degrees for about 1 hour or until set.

Fudgesicles

2 cups pudding (pg. 38)
½ cup milk

Prepare pudding according to directions. Stir in milk, and beat until smooth. • Pour mixture into ice cube trays or small plastic cups. Insert plastic spoons and freeze until solid.

Tomato Strata

½ small loaf of bread, cut into 1-inch cubes
½ cup canned tomatoes, or 1 large tomato, cored and diced
1 cup shredded cheese*
½ tsp. Italian seasoning, or equal amounts oregano, thyme, and
    rosemary
1–2 cups milk
4–5 eggs
salt and pepper to taste

Grease a 9x13-inch baking dish. • Toss together bread, tomato, seasonings, and cheese. Spread evenly in prepared dish. • Whisk together eggs, milk, and salt and pepper. Pour evenly over bread mixture. (You may need a bit more milk. The bread should be soaked to the top.) • Cover with plastic wrap and refrigerate at least 2 hours or overnight. • Bake at 425 degrees for 30 minutes.

*If using powdered cheese, make a paste to equal 1 cup.

Spaghetti Sauce

2–3 qts. tomatoes, drained
¼ tsp. garlic salt
1 tsp. oregano
3 tsp. Italian seasoning
1½ tsp. sugar
1 tsp. salt
1 tsp. chili powder
⅛ tsp. cayenne pepper
⅛ tsp. curry powder

In a saucepan, cook tomatoes down to a sauce of desired thickness. Add remaining ingredients. • Simmer 1–2 hours.

Makes 4 cups sauce.

Pizza Sauce

Makes a wonderful dip for pizza crust strips.

3 large cans tomatoes
½ cup chopped onion
½ cup tomato sauce (pg. 34)
1 clove garlic
2 tsp. sugar
½ tsp. oregano
2 tsp. salt
¼ tsp. pepper
¼ tsp. basil
¼ tsp. nutmeg
¼ tsp. parsley flakes

Place all ingredients in a saucepan and simmer uncovered, stirring occasionally, for 2 hours or more.

Magic Mix

4 cups instant powdered milk, or 2⅓ cups milk
1 cup flour, or ½ cup cornstarch
1 cup (2 sticks) margarine or butter

Combine milk, flour, and margarine in large bowl and mix until it looks like cornmeal. • Keep mix tightly covered in the refrigerator.

Makes 5 cups Magic Mix.

White Sauce

Use Magic Mix for all recipes calling for a white sauce.

²/₃ cup Magic Mix (pg. 37)
1 cup cold water

In saucepan combine Magic Mix and cold water. Stir rapidly over medium heat until it starts to bubble.

Makes 1 cup.

Macaroni & Cheese

1 cup white sauce from Magic Mix (above)
1 cup uncooked macaroni or noodles (pg. 26–27)
4–5 oz. (1 cup) shredded cheese, or powdered cheese prepared according to directions on package
½–1 tsp. salt or garlic salt

Cook macaroni in boiling water until tender. Drain. • Combine macaroni, white sauce, cheese, and seasoning. Heat through.

Serves 4.

Classic Pudding

½ cup sugar
2–3 Tbsp. cocoa (optional)
1 cup Magic Mix (pg. 37)
2 cups water
1 tsp. vanilla

Combine Magic Mix, sugar, and cocoa in saucepan. Mix well. • Add water; stir over medium heat until pudding bubbles. Add vanilla and beat. • Cover and cool.

Makes four ½-cup servings.

Bread Pudding

2½ cups dry bread cubes
⅓ cups raisins (optional)
4 eggs
2 cups milk
⅓ cup sugar
½ tsp. cinnamon
½ tsp. vanilla
¼ tsp. salt

Place bread cubes in 8x2-inch round baking dish. If desired, sprinkle raisins over bread. • Beat together remaining ingredients and pour mixture over bread. • Bake at 325 degrees for 40–45 minutes or till a knife inserted near center comes out clean. Cool slightly.

Makes 6 servings.

Step 4

Now add:
    Unflavored gelatin
    Canned milk
    Canned fruits

Crunchy Wheat Pie Crust
• •

1⅓ cups Crunchy Wheat crumbs (see Crunchy Wheat Cereal,
    pg. 25)
2 Tbsp. sugar
⅓ cup melted margarine

Using the finer crumbs sifted from the Crunchy Wheat
cereal, combine all ingredients. Mix well and press firmly
against sides and bottom of pie tin. • Pour filling into the
shell and refrigerate until firmly set.

Egg Substitute
• •

This is a great substitute to use in baking.

1 tsp. unflavored gelatin
3 Tbsp. cold water
2 Tbsp. plus 1 tsp. boiling water

Combine all ingredients.

This mixture will substitute for 1 egg in a recipe.

Amazing Lemon Cream Pie Filling

2 cups plus 2 Tbsp. water, divided
dash of salt
⅓ cup wheat flour
⅓ cup powdered milk
⅔ cup sugar
1 tsp. gelatin
1 pkg. lemonade Kool-Aid without sugar

Bring to boil 1 cup of water and salt. • Make a paste with ½ cup water and wheat flour. Slowly pour mixture into boiling water, stirring constantly. Let cook on low heat for 7–8 minutes, stirring frequently. Remove from heat. • In small mixing bowl, combine powdered milk powder, sugar, and ½ cup cold water. Set aside. • Soften gelatin in 2 Tbsp. cold water, put on low heat, and stir until dissolved. Add gelatin to milk mixture and stir until thoroughly mixed. Add Kool-Aid. Mix until dissolved. Combine with water and wheat flour mixture and mix well. • Pour into 8-inch Crunchy Wheat pie crust (pg. 40) and serve with Powdered Milk Dream Whip (pg. 43).

Variations:
• Chocolate Cream Pie: Follow directions for lemon pie, except add 1 Tbsp. cocoa and ½ tsp. vanilla instead of lemonade.
• Pudding: Add ¼ cup milk to pie filling recipe, and blend in blender.

Fruit Smoothie
• •

This is a good way to use bottled or canned fruit.

2 cups bottled or canned fruit with juice
¾ cup water
4 Tbsp. nonfat powdered milk
1–2 drops almond flavoring or 1 Tbsp. lemon juice (optional)
7–8 ice cubes

Put in blender and blend until smooth. • Add ice cubes and blend until smooth.

Variation:
• If using fresh fruit: Use 1 cup of fruit and 1 cup water and sweeten to taste. Almond flavoring works well with cherries and large pitted fruits; lemon juice with berries.

Natural Fruit Juice Knox Blox
• •

4 envelopes unflavored gelatin
1 cup cold fruit juice (from canned fruit)
3 cups fruit juice heated to boiling

In a bowl, sprinkle gelatin over cold juice. Let stand 1 minute. Add hot juice and stir until gelatin is completely dissolved. • Pour into a 9x13-inch dish and chill until firm. Cut into 1-inch squares.

Variation
Jell-O fruit salad: Follow the directions above, except use 2 envelopes of Knox and add the fruit to the mixture before chilling. Top with Dream Whip (pg. 43) or whipped evaporated milk (pg. 20).

Powdered Milk Dream Whip (Whipped Cream)

1 cup milk
1½ Tbsp. cold water, divided
2 tsp. gelatin
¼ cup sugar
1 tsp. vanilla

Dissolve gelatin in 1½ Tbsp cold water. Combine mixture with milk and sugar. Place in the refrigerator and stir occasionally until gelled. • Beat mixture until it reaches the consistency of whipped cream. Add vanilla and beat again.

Fruit Smoothie Jell-O Salad

1 cup fruit smoothie (pg. 42), cold
1 cup fruit smoothie, heated to boiling
1 envelope unflavored gelatin

In a bowl, sprinkle gelatin over cold juice; let stand 1 minute. Add hot juice and stir until gelatin is completely dissolved. • Pour into 9x9-inch dish and chill in fridge until firm. Top with whipped evaporated milk (see p.20).

Topping for Jell-O Salad

½ cup sugar
2 Tbsp. flour
1 cup fruit juice or juice drained from canned fruit
1 egg

Beat sugar, flour, and egg together until creamy. Add juice and cook over medium high heat until thick. Cool. • Fold in 1 recipe of the dream whip (above). Spread on top of set Jell-O.

Baby Formula

	Baby's First Formula	Baby's Second Formula	Baby's Third Formula
Evaporated Milk	6 oz.	10 oz.	13 oz.
Water, boiled	10 oz.	15 oz.	19 oz.
Sugar or Corn syrup	1½ Tbsp.	2½ Tbsp.	3 Tbsp.

Gradually shift from the first formula to the third formula over the first 4 months, increasing the amount as your baby grows. • After this, if the baby is gaining weight and eating solids, you would give undiluted whole milk or evaporated milk diluted with equal parts of water, and omit the sugar.

Step 5

Now add:
   Soup base
   Rice
   Legumes/beans
   Alfalfa seeds
   Sesame seeds
   Meats

Chili Beans

2 cups dry beans (kidney or pinto)
1 tsp. salt
4 cups boiling water
2 Tbsp. sugar
1 onion, chopped (optional)
1 Tbsp. chili powder
1 cup tomato sauce (pg. 34) or ketchup
1 tsp. dry mustard

Soak beans overnight. Drain and add other ingredients. Cook for ½ hour on top of stove. • Transfer to slow cooker and cook at 200–250 degrees for 3 hours, or continue to cook on the stove but turn heat down and use a heavy saucepan. • Cook until beans are tender. You could also add soybeans for protein.

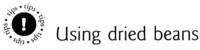 ## Using dried beans

Soaking and cooking beans before mixing with other recipe ingredients helps to get the right tenderness and can minimize final cooking time. Adding 1 Tbsp. oil will cut down on foam as beans cook. Stored beans should be rotated regularly. They continue to lose moisture and will not reconstitute well if kept too long.

Overnight soaking
For each 1 lb. beans, dissolve 2 tsp. salt in 6 cups water. Wash beans, add to salted water, and soak overnight.

Quick soaking
For each 1 lb. beans, bring 8 cups water to a boil. Wash beans, add to boiling water, and boil for 2 minutes. Remove from heat, cover, and soak 1 hour.

Cooking soaked beans
1 lb. (2½ cups) dry beans = 6–7 cups cooked
For each 1 lb. dried beans, dissolve 2 tsp. salt in 6 cups boiling water. Add soaked beans and boil gently, uncovered, adding water if needed to keep beans covered until tender.

Cooking old or hard beans
Wash and sort to remove any discolored beans or foreign material. For each cup dry beans, add 2½ cups hot tap water and 2 tsp. baking soda and soak overnight. Drain and rinse twice, add water to cover, and cook until tender and soft, about 2 hours, adding more water as needed.

 Replacing oil with white beans in most baking

• Cover beans with water and cook until very soft. Mash until consistency of shortening (use blender). Replace in recipes cup for cup. (For example, if a recipe calls for 1 cup margarine, use 1 cup mashed beans.) • Liquid may be added to adjust the consistency. Mashed beans do not keep long in the fridge, so freeze them.

Basic Split Pea Soup

1 cup split peas
5 cups water and 5 chicken bouillon cubes or 3 cans of broth
and 2 cans of water

Any combination of the following:
2 cups chopped luncheon pork sausage
1 small diced onion
2 cloves garlic
1 Tbsp. Worcestershire sauce
2 tsp. salt
⅛ tsp. rosemary
¼ tsp. pepper

Simmer peas in broth about 45 minutes or until peas are tender. When slightly cooled, pour into a blender and add the desired ingredients. Blend until it reaches desired consistency. Return the soup to saucepan and heat. • Rinse blender with small amount of water. Add water from blender to soup. • Simmer about 10 minutes.

Lentil Soup

1½ quarts water and 6 chicken bouillon cubes or 3 (14.5-oz.)
   cans chicken broth and 3 cans of water
1 large can stewed tomatoes
1 bay leaf
3 carrots, cut in chunks (optional)
2 cups lentils
salt and pepper to taste
1 onion, cut up (optional)
1 lb. cooked hamburger or soybeans

Put all ingredients except hamburger in a 4-quart kettle, and bring to a boil. Let cook until lentils are tender. • Add cooked meat.

Using rice

- Cook rice in beef or chicken broth or in water. Mix cooked rice with a variety of things—sliced mushrooms, sautéed onions, crumbled pieces of bacon, slivered almonds, or shredded cheese. Try mixing sour cream and chives into rice.
- Substitute ½ cup fruit juice (orange, apple, and cherry) for ½ cup water when cooking. Vegetable juice cocktail or tomato juice may also be exchanged for 1 cup of the water used in cooking.
- Add 1 of the following herbs to the cooking water when preparing rice:

  ⅛ tsp. dried thyme, oregano, sage, rosemary, or basil

  ½ tsp. celery seeds or dried dill

  seasoned salt instead of salt

  ¾ tsp. dried marjoram

  1 small bay leaf

Steamed Rice

2 cups water
1 cup rice
1 tsp. salt

Wash rice in water and drain. Add 2 cups water and salt. Bring to a boil, then turn down to simmer for 15 minutes. • Turn off and let steam another 5–10 minutes until moisture is absorbed.

Variations:
- Stir in raisins, milk, sugar, and cinnamon for a dessert.
- Stir in butter or margarine until melted.

Makes 4 servings.

Red Beans & Rice

1 lb. red kidney beans
8–10 cups water
½ lb. hamburger or soybeans, cooked
1 minced clove of garlic
1 onion, chopped (fresh or dried)
2 Tbsp. parsley
2 large bay leaves
chopped green pepper,
creole seasoning salt
cayenne pepper
salt to taste.

Sort and rinse beans. Cover with water and bring to a boil. Boil for 2 minutes. Remove from heat, cover and let stand for 1 hour. • Rinse beans. Cover with 8–10 cups water and begin heating. • In a separate pan, brown meat and sauté vegetables and garlic. Add to beans with remaining ingredients. Simmer for about 2–4 hours. • Serve over rice. 1 lb. (2½ cups) dry beans = 6–7 cups cooked

Spanish Fried Rice

2 Tbsp. oil
2 cups rice
1 cup chopped onion (fresh or dried)
4 cups water
2 cups tomato sauce
2 Tbsp. chili powder

Put oil in frying pan; heat to very hot. Add rice and chopped onion; stir until rice starts to brown. Slowly add water and chili powder. • Simmer for 20 minutes. Add tomato sauce. Stir and serve.

Makes 8–10 servings.

Baked Rice Pudding

4 cups milk, divided
3 eggs, beaten
½ cup long grain rice
2 cups milk
½ cup raisins (optional)
¼ cup butter or margarine
½ cup sugar
1 tsp. vanilla
½ tsp. salt
nutmeg or cinnamon

In a heavy medium saucepan, bring 2 cups of milk, uncooked rice, and raisins to boil; reduce heat. Cover and cook over very low heat about 15 minutes or until rice is tender. Remove from heat. Stir in butter or margarine until melted. • In a mixing bowl, stir together eggs, 2 cups of milk, sugar, vanilla, and salt. • Gradually stir rice mixture into egg mixture. Pour into a 10x6x2-inch baking dish. Bake in a 325-degree oven for 30 minutes. • Stir well, and sprinkle with nutmeg or cinnamon. Bake for another 15–20 minutes or until knife inserted in the center comes out clean. Serve warm or chilled with cream or milk.

Makes 6 servings.

Refried Beans

2 cups cooked pinto beans
2 Tbsp. oil
salt to taste

Heat oil in a frying pan. • Mash the beans and add the salt. • Add beans to pan. Mix well.

Step 6

Now add (fresh, frozen, canned, or dried):
  Vegetables
  Potatoes

Creamy Soup

4 cups water
2 cups Magic Mix (see pg. 37)
1 cube or 1 tsp. bouillon

Any combination of the following:
3 cups carrots, mashed
1 Tbsp. onion, cooked and chopped
3 potatoes, cooked and chopped
1 pkg. chopped spinach, cooked
1 can clams, chopped
1 can cream-style corn

Combine water, Magic Mix, and bouillon in saucepan. Stir over medium heat until slightly thick. Add desired ingredients. Heat thoroughly.

Tuna Noodle Casserole

Add 1 can of tuna (or any type of canned meat) to the Pasta and Cheese Casserole (pg. 35).

Pasta Salad

1 cup uncooked macaroni or pasta (pg. 26–27)
1 tsp. salt
4 cups boiling water
1 can tuna
1 cup chopped vegetables (celery, green pepper, onion, sprouts, etc.)
salad dressing or mayonnaise (pg. 26)

Bring water and salt to a boil. Add pasta and cook until tender. Drain. Rinse in cold water and drain again. Chill. • Mix with tuna or other cold meat (crab, shrimp, chicken, salmon, etc.) and vegetables. Marinate with dressing to taste, approximately ⅓ cup.

Creamed Tuna on Rice or Toast

Make a white sauce (see p. 38) and add 1 can of tuna (or any type of canned meat). Season to taste. Serve over toasted bread, biscuits, or steamed rice.

Tuna Spread

1 can tuna
⅓ cup diced celery (optional)
½ cup cooked whole wheat
1 tsp. shredded onion (optional)
½ cup salad dressing or mayonnaise (pg. 26)

Mix all ingredients. • Spread on toast, sandwiches, or chips.

How can I add variety?

• Seasonings and spices are especially important when it comes to basic food storage!

• Beef, chicken, or vegetable bouillon granules are excellent secondary storage items. Wheat and rice (either brown or white) cooked in bouillon, take on wonderful new flavors, as does barley. Bouillon is an excellent base for many soups, sauces, and casseroles.

• Soy sauce, with its Asian flavor, is another excellent seasoning. Fried wheat or rice with fresh vegetables and sprouts is enhanced with soy sauce. It also adds good flavor to a stir-fry or even to some stews, chicken, or fish.

• Legumes respond well to seasoning salts and spice blends like chili powder, curry powder, poultry seasoning, and celery, garlic, and onion salts.

• It will be important to keep some sweet spices on hand, such as cinnamon, nutmeg, cloves, ginger, and allspice. Simple rice pudding, for example, is dependent on such spices for its unique flavor. The simplest cookies and cakes are enhanced as well.

• Cocoa or a cereal drink like Postum are good supplementary items to store along with the basic nonfat powdered milk. Fruit drink powder is a welcome flavor in lean times. Don't forget vanilla, almond, lemon, or maple extract for making pancake syrup. Lemon juice and vinegar should also be included.

• A year's supply of flavorings your family enjoys could make the difference between stark and satisfying eating!

Tuna Mac & Cheese

1 cup white sauce (pg. 38)
1 cup uncooked macaroni or other pasta (pg. 26–27)
½ cup reconstituted powdered cheese
½ tsp. salt
1 can of tuna

Cook pasta in boiling water until tender. Drain. • Add the remaining ingredients and heat through.

Easy Fried Rice

3 cups cooked rice (pg. 48)
¼ cup fully cooked pork or ham
¼ cup cooked vegetables

Fry meat in a skillet. Put rice in with meat and soy sauce to taste. Fry for about 5 minutes. • Stir and fry for another 5 minutes. Add cooked vegetables.

Cheesy Potato Casserole

2 cups dried potatoes
2 Tbsp. powdered butter
4 Tbsp. milk powder
1 cup water
2 Tbsp. powdered cheese
2 Tbsp. bread crumbs

Cook potatoes in 6 cups boiling water and 1 tsp. salt until tender. Drain and add other ingredients. Blend well and place in a greased 9x13-inch baking dish. • Top with buttered bread crumbs and bake at 350 degrees for about 20 minutes or until heated through.

Variation:
Try adding canned tuna, salmon, clams, or Spam.

Cream of Potato Soup

1½ cups chicken broth
1 Tbsp. dry onion
2 Tbsp. butter or margarine
2 Tbsp. flour
¼ tsp. salt
dash of pepper
1 cup sliced potatoes
1 cup milk
seasonings as desired (recommendation: ½ tsp. dry dill weed)

In a saucepan, combine chicken broth, onion, potatoes, and seasonings (add more water if potatoes are dehydrated—read package instructions and make adjustments). Bring to a boil and simmer for 5–10 minutes or until potatoes are tender. • Remove from heat and place half of it in a blender or food processor. Cover and blend until smooth. Repeat with remaining mixture and set aside. • In the same saucepan, melt the butter. Blend in flour, salt, and pepper. Add the milk all at once. Cook and stir until mixture is thickened and bubbly. • Stir in the blended vegetable mixture. Cook and stir until soup is heated through. Season to taste with additional salt and pepper.

Variations:
• Chunky potato soup: Do not blend vegetable mixture.
• Clams can be added to this too.
• Potato cheese soup: Add reconstituted powdered cheese or 8 oz. Velveeta cheese as desired. Taste often to get it just right.

Salmon Loaf

I can salmon, drained
I egg, slightly beaten
I Tbsp. lemon juice
⅓ cup dry bread crumbs
¼ tsp. salt
½ cup hot milk
¼ tsp. pepper

Combine all ingredients well and place in a greased baking dish. • Bake at 325 degrees for 30 minutes.

Step 7

Finally, add:
Oats, raisins, nuts, chocolate powder, peanut butter, granola, juices, soup mixes, coconut, corn meal, lemon powder or juice, shortening or margarine, rennet tablet, molasses, corn syrup, vinegar, raw bran, cereals, potato pearls, and condiments.

2-hour Whole Wheat Bread
. . . .

5 cups warm water
2 Tbsp. yeast
⅓ cup honey
⅓ cup oil
2 eggs
⅓ cup potato flakes
6 cups whole wheat flour
1 Tbsp. salt
4-5 cups unbleached flour

Dissolve yeast according to package instructions. Mix all ingredients, except 2 cups of flour, to a spongy consistency. Use a bread mixer or handheld electric beaters. Let rest about 10 minutes. • Add remaining flour gradually as needed to make a soft dough. Knead on floured board; cover with plastic wrap and let rise until double. • Punch down, shape into four loaves, and place in greased bread pans. Cover and let rise again until double. • Bake at 350 degrees for 30–40 minutes. Put hot bread on a towel to cool for a soft crust.

Makes 4 loaves.

Corn Bread

1²⁄₃ cups flour
²⁄₃ cup sugar
5 tsp. baking powder
1 tsp. salt
1²⁄₃ cups yellow cornmeal
2 eggs, beaten
⅓ cup margarine, melted
1²⁄₃ cups milk

Mix flour, sugar, baking powder, and salt in a large bowl. Stir in cornmeal until well blended. Add eggs and milk and stir to a smooth batter. Stir in melted butter just until blended. Do not over stir. • Pour into well-buttered 9x5x3-inch loaf pan. Bake at 425 degrees for 40–50 minutes or until toothpick inserted in center comes out clean. • Cool in pan 10 minutes. Loosen around edges and turn out to cool.

Honey Butter

½ cup butter or margarine, softened
½ cup honey
¼ tsp. vanilla

Whip butter or margarine, then add vanilla. Add honey gradually while whipping.

Makes 1 cup.

Oatmeal Bread

½ cup warm water
2 Tbsp. active dry yeast
¾ cup water, boiling
¾ cup rolled oats
½ cup honey or molasses
⅓ cup vegetable oil
2 cups flour
1 Tbsp. salt
3-3½ cups flour
½ tsp. baking soda
1 cup buttermilk (pg. 109)

In small bowl, stir yeast into the ½ cup warm water. Allow to stand until yeast dissolves and bubbles up. • In medium saucepan, bring ¾ cup water to boil; stir in oatmeal and cook several minutes. Remove from heat; add buttermilk, oil, and honey or molasses. • Sift 2 cups flour, salt, and baking soda into a large mixing bowl. Add yeast mixture and oats mixture and beat with wire whip or slotted spoon; let stand 5 minutes. • Gradually add enough of remaining flour until dough is stiff enough for kneading. Turn out onto floured surface and knead 8–10 minutes or until a soft, elastic ball forms.

Place dough in clean, greased bowl and cover with plastic wrap. • Allow to rise until double in size, about 1½ hours. Punch dough down and divide into two portions; cover with bowl or towel and allow to rest 10 minutes. • Form into two loaves and place in greased 8x4-inch pans. Cover and let rise until double in size. • Bake at 350–375 degrees for 45–50 minutes or until done. Remove from oven and turn out to cool on wire rack.

Makes 2 loaves.

Oatmeal Raisin Muffins

3 tsp. baking powder
1 egg
½ tsp. salt
¾ cup milk
½ tsp. nutmeg
½ cup vegetable oil
¼ tsp. cinnamon
⅓ cup sugar
1 cup white or whole wheat flour
1 cup raisins (optional)

Heat oven to 400 degrees. Grease bottoms only of 12 medium muffin cups or line with cupcake liners. • Beat egg, and stir in milk, raisins, and oil. Stir in remaining ingredients all at once just until flour is moistened (batter will be lumpy). • Fill muffin cups about ¾ full. Bake until golden brown, about 20 minutes. Remove from pan immediately.

Never-Fail Pie Crust

2½ cups flour
1 egg, beaten
½ tsp. vinegar
1 tsp. salt
1 cup shortening, heaping
water

Cut flour, salt, and shortening together until it reaches the consistency of oatmeal. Put egg in measuring cup and add water to make ½ cup. Whip together with vinegar until foamy, then add to the flour mixture. Mix completely. • Divide into 2 (3-inch) balls. Roll out with small amount of flour to avoid sticking.

Makes 3 single crusts.

Sourdough Starter

1 (1-Tbsp.) package dry yeast
2½ cups water, divided
2 cups flour
1 tablespoon sugar

Dissolve yeast in ½ cup warm water, allow to rest 10 minutes. • Mix in flour, sugar, and remaining 2 cups water. • Allow to stand, loosely covered, in a warm place for 3 to 4 days. Use a large (non-metal) bowl as it will rise considerably. • Keep covered in the fridge between uses. • To make it into a basic dough, add another 2 cups flour and 2 cups warm water, then allow to stand at room temperature overnight. • Don't forget to reserve a cup of the starter for future use.

Sourdough Bread

1 package dry yeast
2 Tbsp. sugar
1½ cups Sourdough Starter (above)
2 tsp. salt
3½–4 cups flour
1 egg
1 cup warm water

Mix starter, yeast, and 1 cup warm water. Let stand until yeast is dissolved. Add remaining ingredients, except egg. Let it rise and punch down. • Form into loaves. Cover and let rise until doubled. Beat egg and brush over unbaked loaves. Bake at 400 degrees for 30–35 minutes.

Sourdough English Muffins

2 cups Sourdough Starter (pg. 61)
6 Tbsp. yellow cornmeal
¾ cup buttermilk
I tsp. baking soda
2¾–3 cups flour
¼ tsp. salt

Mix together Sourdough Starter and buttermilk. Combine flour, 4 Tbsp. of the cornmeal, soda, and salt. Add this mixture to the buttermilk mixture. Stir to combine, using hands when necessary. • Turn onto lightly floured surface and knead until smooth, adding more flour if necessary. Roll dough to ⅔-inch thickness. Cover and let rise a few minutes. • Using a 3-inch cutter, cut muffins. Sprinkle sheet of waxed paper with the remaining cornmeal. Place the cut muffins on this and cover. Let rise until very light, about 45 minutes. • Bake on medium hot, lightly greased griddle about 30 minutes, turning often. Cool and slice. • Toast and serve with butter.

Makes 12–14 muffins.

Cooked Rolled Oats

I tsp. salt
4 cups water
2 cups quick-cooking rolled oats

Put water and salt in pan and heat to boiling. Slowly stir in rolled oats. • Cook slowly for 1 minute, stirring to keep from sticking. Remove from heat. Cover and let stand a few minutes.

Basic Pancake or Waffle Batter

3 cups milk (or buttermilk)
3 eggs
1½ cups whole wheat flour
2 tsp. salt
1½ tsp. baking powder
3 Tbsp. sugar
⅓ cup applesauce
1½ cups flour

Mix well and cook. Top with maple syrup (pg. 30, 64)

Delicious Oatmeal Pancakes

½ cup whole wheat flour
¼ tsp. salt
2 tsp. baking powder
2 Tbsp. sugar
⅓ cup nonfat powdered milk
2 eggs, separated
3 Tbsp. oil
1 cup water
1 cup rolled oats

In medium bowl, combine flour, baking powder, salt, sugar, and powdered milk; stir until well blended. • In small bowl, beat egg whites until stiff; set aside. • In large mixing bowl, combine egg yolks, water, oil, and oats; beat slightly and allow to stand 5 minutes, then beat until blended. • Mix in dry ingredients, then fold in beaten egg whites. For small pancakes, drop 2 Tbsp. batter onto griddle or pour ¼ measuring cup full, if larger pancakes are desired. • Cook until cakes are full of bubbles on top and undersides are lightly browned. Turn with spatula and brown other side. Serve with applesauce, jam, or maple syrup (pg. 30, 64).

Makes 8–10 pancakes.

Deluxe Maple Syrup

1 cup white sugar
1 cup brown sugar
1 cup light corn syrup
1 cup water
2 tsp. maple or 1 tsp. vanilla and 1 tsp. maple

Combine all ingredients except the flavorings. Bring to
a boil and boil for 5 minutes. Remove from heat and cool
slightly. Add flavorings and transfer to a syrup container.

Mountain Breakfast Meal

1 cup cracked wheat (pg. 13)
3 cups water
1 tsp. salt
1 tsp. butter
⅓ cup honey
⅓ cup raisins

Mix all ingredients in a saucepan. Bring to a rolling boil
for 2 minutes, stirring occasionally. Cover and remove from
the burner. • Let sit for 2–3 hours or overnight for the best
taste and texture. In the morning, reheat or eat cold with or
without milk.

Granola

6 cups rolled oats
½ cup brown sugar
1 cup coconut
⅓ cup sesame seeds
1 cup chopped nuts
¼ cup sunflower seeds
½ cup raisins or other dried fruit
½ cup oil
⅓ cup honey
2 tsp. vanilla

Mix all dry ingredients except raisins. Stir in oil, honey, and vanilla, and coat thoroughly. • Spread on cookie sheet and bake at 350 degrees for 30 minutes (stir about every 10 minutes during baking). • In the last 5 minutes add raisins or other dried fruit.

Makes about 2 quarts.

Macaroni Salad

1 cup uncooked macaroni
1 tsp. salt
4 cups boiling water
1 can tuna
1 cup chopped vegetables (celery, green pepper, onion, cooked peas, carrots, etc.)
salad dressing

Bring water and salt to a boil. Add macaroni. Boil until tender (about 10 minutes); do not over cook. Drain. Rinse in cold water, and drain again. Chill. • Mix with tuna and vegetables. Marinate with salad dressing to taste (approximately ⅓ cup).

Makes 6 servings.

Chinese Fried Wheat

1 cup cracked wheat (pg. 13)
2½ cups flour
½ tsp. salt
3 Tbsp. oil
1 egg, beaten
1 onion, minced
¼ cup celery, diced
2 Tbsp. soy sauce or to taste
bacon or ham

Bring wheat, water, and salt to a boil and cook for 20–30 minutes. Put in a strainer and drain off thick liquid (save for gravy). Wash wheat with cold water to make it fluffy. Press wheat to remove all moisture possible. Set aside. • Heat 1 Tbsp. oil in heavy skillet. In separate bowl, beat egg, stirring rapidly with fork so egg is light and fluffy. Set aside. • Add to skillet 2 Tbsp. oil, minced onion, and celery. Cook until tender. Then add wheat, soy sauce, bacon or ham, and egg. Heat through and serve with extra soy sauce if desired.

Italian Fried Wheat

1 cup cracked wheat (pg. 13)
2 Tbsp. oil
Italian seasonings to taste
salt to taste
leftover roast or other meat, chopped

Prepare wheat the same as for Chinese Fried Wheat above. • Heat oil in skillet and add wheat, Italian seasonings, leftover roast, and salt to taste.

Spanish Fried Wheat

1 onion, chopped
1 cup cracked wheat (pg. 13)
green onions, chopped
salt
beef bouillon powder
chili powder

Prepare wheat the same as for Chinese Fried Wheat (pg. 66).
• Heat oil in skillet, cook chopped onion until golden brown,
then add wheat. Toss lightly. Add remaining ingredients.

Makes 8 servings.

Browned Rice

1 cup uncooked rice
¼ cup shortening
¼ cup chopped meat, onion, celery, or other vegetables
3½ cups water
1 tsp. salt

Heat shortening in skillet. Add rice. Cook, stirring
constantly, about 10 minutes or until lightly browned. • Add
vegetables (optional) and continue cooking 2 or 3 minutes. •
Add salt and water. Simmer over low heat 20–25 minutes or
until rice is tender and excess liquid has evaporated.

Makes 6–8 servings.

Barbecued Lima Beans

2 cups large dried lima beans
8 cups water
¼ lb. bacon, cut into ½-inch pieces, precooked
1 clove garlic, minced
1 small onion, chopped
1 tsp. mustard
½ cup margarine
2 tsp. Worcestershire sauce
1½ tsp. chili powder
1 (8-oz.) can tomato sauce
2 Tbsp. brown sugar
2 Tbsp. vinegar

Sort and rinse beans; do not soak. In 4-qt. saucepan, combine rinsed beans, water, and bacon. Bring to a boil; reduce heat. Cover and simmer until beans are almost tender (1–1½ hours), checking several times. • Add hot water as needed to keep beans just covered while cooking. Drain, reserving ½ cup liquid. • Cook onion and garlic in margarine until soft. Add remaining ingredients except drained lima beans and bacon slices. Cook 5 minutes, then add lima beans. • Place in greased 2-quart casserole dish; top with sliced bacon. Cover and bake for 2 hours at 350 degrees, adding reserved bean liquid if necessary.

Makes 8–10 servings.

Tamale Pie

1 lb. hamburger
1 onion, chopped
1 cup chopped green pepper
1 clove garlic, minced
1 (16-oz.) can tomatoes
1 Tbsp. sugar
1 (6-oz.) can tomato paste
2–3 tsp. chili powder
1 can sliced ripe olives (optional)
1 tsp. salt
1 (12-oz.) can corn, drained
dash of pepper
1 cup shredded cheddar cheese

Brown the hamburger, onion, green pepper, and garlic together. Drain the fat, and add tomatoes, tomato paste, corn, olives, sugar, salt, chili powder, and pepper. • Simmer 20 minutes until thick. Add cheese and stir until melted. Pour into 9x13-inch greased baking dish.

Topping:
¾ cup cornmeal
½ tsp. salt
1½ cups shredded sharp cheddar cheese
1 Tbsp. butter
2 cups cold milk

Heat milk in double boiler; add salt and slowly stir in cornmeal. Cook and stir until thick (about 20 minutes). Add butter. Spread over top of meat mixture. • Bake at 375 degrees for 40 minutes.

Makes 8–10 servings.

Pioneer Stew

1¼ cups (½ lb.) dried pinto or kidney beans
3 cups plus 2 Tbsp. cold water, divided
1 tsp. salt
½–1 lb. ground beef
½ cup chopped onion
½ cup finely diced green pepper
½ tsp. chili powder
1 (16-oz.) can whole kernel corn, with juice
¾ tsp. salt
½ cup shredded sharp cheddar cheese
1 (16-oz.) can tomatoes, with juice
1 Tbsp. flour

In large saucepan, combine washed and drained beans, cold water, and salt. Bring to a boil. Cover and simmer 2 minutes. Remove from heat and let stand for 1 hour. Return to heat and simmer 1 hour and 15 minutes. • In skillet, cook ground beef, onion, and green pepper until meat is browned and vegetables are tender. Drain off fat. • Add meat mixture, corn, tomatoes, chili powder, and salt to taste to beans. Simmer 20 minutes. • Combine 1 Tbsp. flour with 2 Tbsp. water. Stir into stew, cook (while stirring) until thickened and bubbly. Stir in cheese.

Makes 8 servings.

Rice Pilaf

2 cups uncooked rice
⅔ stick margarine
4 cups broth
salt and pepper to taste
¾ cup chopped celery
¾ cup chopped carrots
¾ cup chopped green onions
1 cup slivered almonds

Brown rice lightly with butter in skillet. Place in casserole dish with boiling broth. Cover and bake for 30 minutes at 375 degrees. • Take from oven and add vegetables and almonds, stirring and mixing well with a fork. Return to oven for 30 minutes.

Makes 8 servings.

Beef & Lentil Soup

1½ qts. chicken broth
2 cups lentils
1 large can stewed tomatoes
1 bay leaf
3 carrots, cut in chunks
1 onion, cut up
1 lb. cooked hamburger
salt and pepper to taste

Put all ingredients except hamburger in a 4-quart kettle; bring to a boil and let cook until tender. Add cooked hamburger and heat. • A ham hock may be cooked with above ingredients instead of hamburger, or pieces of ham may be added last.

Makes 8–10 servings.

Cracked Wheat Casserole

1 lb. ground beef
½ cup chopped onion
1 small garlic clove
1½ cups water
½ cup cooked cracked wheat (pg. 13)
2 Tbsp. chopped parsley
1 tsp. beef bouillon
½ tsp. salt
¼ tsp. oregano leaves
¼ tsp. pepper
¼ cup parmesan cheese
1 cup chopped tomato (fresh or canned)

Brown beef with onion and garlic until the pink color has gone from the meat. Drain. Combine with remaining ingredients, except cheese and tomato. • Bake in tightly covered 1½-qt. casserole dish for 45 minutes or until the cracked wheat is tender and the water has been absorbed. • Stir in cheese and tomato; let stand a few minutes and serve.

Makes 6 servings.

Split Pea Soup with Sausage

1 lb. (2¼ cups) green split peas
3 quarts water
½ tsp. pepper
2 tsp. salt
1 lb. bulk pork sausage
¼ tsp. marjoram
1 cup diced potatoes
1 cup diced celery
1 cup diced carrots
1 cup diced onion
salt to taste

Wash and drain split peas. In large saucepan, combine water and seasonings and bring to a boil. Add peas gradually so water does not stop boiling. • Shape sausage into 1-inch balls (about 28 of them) and roll in flour. (You may wish to cook and drain sausage before adding it to the soup.) Drop into soup, cover, and simmer until sausage is well done and peas are tender. • About 20 minutes before time to serve, add vegetables and cook until tender.

Makes 12 servings.

Basic Mexican Salsa

1 quart canned diced tomatoes
1 (14-oz.) can Mexican stewed tomatoes
1–2 cans of diced green chilies
2–3 finely chopped green onions
½ tsp. chili flakes
½ tsp. seasoned salt
garlic salt and black pepper to taste
a pinch of oregano and cumin

Cut up stewed tomatoes. Combine all ingredients.

Cream of Split Pea Soup

4½ cups boiling water
2 cups split peas
½ cup celery, diced
½ cup carrots, diced
1 onion, chopped
2 tsp. salt
2½ cups milk or ⅔ cup powdered milk and 2½ cups water
seasonings to taste
diced ham, bacon, or other meat (optional)

Wash split peas and sort out bad peas. In large saucepan, combine water, split peas, vegetables, and salt. Simmer until peas are soft, about 45 minutes, stirring occasionally. Put through a sieve or a blender. • Add milk, seasonings, and meat, then reheat and serve.

Makes 8 servings.

Delicious Turkey Soup with Dry Soup Mix

8 cups chicken or turkey broth, or reconstituted chicken bouillon
salt and pepper to taste
1 cup diced celery
2 cups diced turkey or chicken
¾ cup dry soup mix
1 large can evaporated milk

Mix broth, soup mix, salt and pepper, and celery. Simmer for 45 minutes. • Stir in diced turkey and evaporated milk. Heat and serve. Add flour or cornstarch to thicken.

Makes 6 servings.

Gluten Roast

2 cups raw gluten (pg. 16)
½ cup walnuts
¼ cup soy sauce
½ tsp. salt
1 tsp. onion powder
⅛ tsp. pepper
¼ cup ketchup
1 Tbsp. water

Grind gluten and nuts together in a food grinder. Add soy sauce, salt, onion powder, and pepper. Mix. Shape into a loaf in a baking pan. • Combine ketchup and water. Spread over top of loaf. Bake at 350 degrees for 1 hour and 15 minutes.

Gluten Meat Extender

Add beef bouillon granules to raw gluten (see pg. 16) and knead in. Use about 1 tsp. granules per ½ lb. raw gluten. • Stretch mixture onto a well-oiled cookie sheet. Bake at 300 degrees for about 20 minutes or until dry. Grind. Use equal parts ground beef and extender in your favorite recipe.

Hamburger Soup

2 cans beef broth and 1 cup water or 4 cups water and 4 bouillon cubes
½ cup soup mix
1 qt. tomato juice (or tomatoes)
season to taste
½ lb. browned, drained hamburger

In large saucepan, combine broth and soup mix. Bring to a boil and simmer for 45 minutes, or until tender. • Add tomatoes or juice and hamburger; simmer 5 minutes. Season to taste; serve.

Sweet & Sour Meatballs

½ lb. ground beef
2 tsp. soy sauce
½ lb. gluten, flavored
½ lb. sausage, ground
1¾ cups milk
I tsp. salt
I clove garlic, minced
I egg
¾ cup cooked cracked wheat
I tsp. ginger
I (5-oz.) can water chestnuts, drained and diced
I (8-oz.) can crushed pineapple, drained (reserve juice)

Combine all ingredients; form into 30 balls. Place in a 9x13-inch baking dish. Bake at 350 degrees for 25 minutes. • Prepare sauce while meatballs are baking.

Sauce:
½ cup brown sugar
2 tsp. soy sauce
I beef bouillon cube, crushed
2 Tbsp. cornstarch
1½ cups liquid (reserved pineapple juice plus other liquid, to make 1½ cups)
½ tsp. salt
3 Tbsp. vinegar

Combine all ingredients. Cook over low heat, stirring constantly, till thickened. • Pour over baked meatballs. Bake another 10 minutes. Serve hot.

Chocolate Chip Oatmeal Cookies

1 cup melted shortening, butter, or margarine
2 eggs
1 tsp. vanilla
⅔ cup granulated sugar
1½ cups flour
⅔ cup brown sugar
½ tsp. soda
1 Tbsp. hot water
2 cups rolled oats
1 (6-oz.) pkg. chocolate chips
½ cup nuts, coarsely chopped

In large bowl, cream shortening. Add sugars and cream until fluffy. Beat in eggs and vanilla. Add flour, salt, and soda that have been dissolved in hot water; blend. Stir in rolled oats, chocolate chips, and nuts. • Drop by teaspoonfuls onto ungreased baking sheet about 1½ inches apart. • Bake at 375 degrees for 10 minutes or until barely brown and still a little puffy. For crisper cookies, bake until cookies flatten.

Makes 3 dozen cookies.

Broiled Coconut Icing

6 Tbsp. (¾ stick) butter or margarine
½ cup brown sugar
¼ cup cream or evaporated milk
¾ cups nuts, coarsely chopped
1 cup coconut

Combine all ingredients. Spread over spice, oatmeal, or carrot cake. • Broil until frosting bubbles and browns slightly, taking care not to burn.

Oatmeal Cake

1¼ cups boiling water
1 cup rolled oats
½ cup butter or margarine
½ tsp. nutmeg
2 eggs, slightly beaten
1 tsp. cinnamon
¾ cup granulated sugar
1 tsp. soda
¾ cup brown sugar
1 tsp. salt
1½ cups sifted flour

Pour boiling water over rolled oats; let stand 20 minutes. • Cream together butter or margarine and sugars. Add eggs. Stir in oatmeal, then sift in dry ingredients. • Bake in greased 9x13-inch pan at 350 degrees for 40–45 minutes or until toothpick inserted in center comes out clean.

Coconut Cream Pie Filling

1 Tbsp. small cracked wheat
¼ tsp. coconut flavoring (or to taste)

Make as for lemon cream pie (pg. 41) except add small cracked wheat (tastes like coconut when finished) to water and wheat flour mixture before cooking. • Add coconut flavoring when all ingredients are mixed together.

Wheat & Raisin Chocolate Chip Cookies

1½ cups margarine or shortening
1½ cups sugar
1½ cups brown sugar
4 eggs
2½ cups whole wheat flour
2 tsp. vanilla
2½ cups all-purpose flour
½ tsp. salt
2 tsp. baking soda
2 Tbsp. hot water
1 cup chopped nuts
1 cup raisins
1 (12-oz.) pkg. chocolate chips

Beat margarine in large bowl until soft. Gradually add sugars, beating until light and fluffy. Add vanilla. Add eggs, 1 at a time, beating well. • Mix both kinds of flour and salt in separate bowl. Gradually add flour mixture to sugar mixture, beating at low speed until well mixed. • Dissolve baking soda in hot water and add to sugar-flour mixture. • Stir in nuts, raisins, and chocolate chips. • Using 1 generous Tbsp. of dough for each cookie, place on greased cookie sheet. • Bake at 350 degrees for 10–12 minutes. Allow to cool.

Graham Crackers

⅓ cup dry powdered milk
½ cup water
1 Tbsp. lemon juice or vinegar
1 cup brown sugar
½ cup honey
2 tsp. vanilla
2 eggs, beaten slightly
6 cups whole wheat flour
1 tsp. salt
1 tsp. soda

Mix milk, water, and lemon juice or vinegar. In separate bowl, add dark brown sugar, honey, vanilla, and eggs (in that order). Blend well to keep oil in emulsion. Combine the two mixtures and add flour, salt, and soda. • Divide into four equal parts. Place each part on a greased and floured cookie sheet. Roll from center to edge until ⅛ inch thick. Prick with a fork. • Bake at 375 degrees for about 15 minutes or until light brown. Remove from oven and cut into squares.

Peanut Butter Candy

1 cup peanut butter
1 lb. powdered sugar
2 sticks margarine, melted
1 cup crushed graham crackers (optional)
1 (6-oz.) pkg. chocolate chips (optional)

Combine everything but the chocolate chips. Roll into balls. Refrigerate until hardened. Eat plain, roll in graham crackers, or dip into melted chocolate chips.

Date-Filled Wheat Cookies

2 cups brown sugar
1 cup shortening
¼–½ cup water
2 eggs
1 tsp. vanilla
1 tsp. salt
1 tsp. baking soda
¼ tsp. cinnamon
1½ cups white flour
2 cups wheat flour

Cream shortening and sugar. Add eggs and vanilla. Mix dry ingredients in another bowl. Alternate dry ingredients and water. • Shape dough into 2 rolls, each about 2 inches in diameter. Refrigerate.

Filling:
2 cups chopped dates (or chopped raisins)
¾ cup sugar
¾ cup water
½ cup chopped nuts

Combine dates, sugar, and water. Cook over low heat until thick. Remove from heat and stir in nuts. Cool. • Slice dough into thin slices and place on cookie sheet; top with 1 tsp. of filling and place another round on top. Don't pinch down. • Bake on ungreased cookie sheet at 375 degrees for 10–12 minutes.

Makes 3 dozen cookies.

Honey Mints

1 cup warm honey
green food coloring
4 drops oil of peppermint
2¾ cups powdered milk (non-instant)

Mix ingredients and knead until all milk is absorbed. Roll into 1-inch balls. Allow to set until firm.

Pinto Bean Fudge

1 cup cooked soft pinto beans, drained and mashed
¼ cup milk
1 Tbsp. vanilla
6 oz. unsweetened chocolate
2 Tbsp. butter or margarine
2 lbs. powdered sugar or to taste
nuts (optional)

In large bowl, stir beans and milk together, adding enough milk for mixture to resemble mashed potatoes; stir in vanilla. • Melt chocolate and butter, and stir into bean mixture. Gradually stir in powdered sugar. Knead with hands to get it well blended. • Spread into lightly buttered 9-inch baking dish or form into 2 (1½-inch) rolls. Chill 1–2 hours.

Oh Harry Bars

½ cup melted margarine
1 tsp. vanilla
½ cup corn syrup
½ cup peanut butter
1 (6-oz.) pkg. chocolate chips
4 cups oats
1 cup brown sugar

Mix together margarine, syrup, vanilla, peanut butter, and brown sugar. Heat until dissolved. Stir in oats and chips. • Press into greased 9x13-inch pan. Bake at 375 degrees for 15 minutes. Don't over bake. Cut into bars.

Chocolate Rolls

1 cup honey
1 tsp. vanilla
1 cup non-instant powdered milk
½ cup cocoa

Cook honey to 255 degrees (hard ball stage). Do not over cook. Remove from heat. Add vanilla. Mix cocoa and powdered milk well and stir into honey. • Pull like taffy until gloss is gone. Shape into rolls.

Classic Pudding

¼ cup milk
lemon, chocolate, or coconut cream pie filling (pg. 41)

Combine milk and pie filling in blender. Beat slightly.

Peanut Butter Snap, Crackle, & Pop

¾ cup powdered sugar
I cup peanut butter
½ cup powdered milk
½ stick margarine
I½ cups crisp rice breakfast cereal
I (6-oz.) pkg. chocolate chips

Mix powdered sugar and powdered milk thoroughly. Add peanut butter and melted margarine. Stir in rice cereal. • Form into walnut-sized pieces. For an added treat, dip in chocolate.

Honey Boy Taffy

2 cups sugar
6 Tbsp. cornstarch
½ tsp. salt
I cup water
I¼ cup honey

Mix the sugar, salt, and cornstarch together; stir in the water and honey. Cook to hard thread stage. Pour onto a buttered cookie sheet. • While mixture cools, fold the edges toward the center so it will cool uniformly. • Butter hands and pull until milky looking. Shape into small rope and cut into 1-inch pieces. Wrap in waxed paper.

Pinto Bean Dip
. . . .

2 cups mashed pinto beans, cooked
1 tsp. seasoned salt
dash of garlic salt or powder
1/8 tsp. cayenne pepper
1/4 cup canned milk
1/4 cup French dressing

Mix all ingredients together and beat until light and creamy.

Pinto Bean Sandwich Spread
. . . .

1 cup mashed pinto beans
1 small onion, minced
1 dill pickle, minced
2 Tbsp. mustard
1 Tbsp. ketchup
salt and pepper to taste

Add beans, onion, and pickle that have been minced. Add mustard, ketchup, salt, and pepper. For creamier spread: Add sweet cream to taste.

Pinto Icebox Cookies
. . . .

3/4 cup shortening
2 eggs
2 cups brown sugar
1/2 tsp. salt
1/4 cup salad dressing
1 tsp. vanilla
3/4 cup cooked, mashed pinto beans
3-4 cups flour

Mix and drop in rounded teaspoons on ungreased cookie sheet bake at 350 degrees until edges are golden brown.

Pinto Bean Bread

2 cups cooked, mashed pinto beans
2 cups milk
2 Tbsp. sugar
6 cups all-purpose flour
2 (I Tbsp.) pkgs. active dry yeast
2 Tbsp. shortening
2 tsp. salt

Sprinkle yeast over lukewarm milk and stir. Blend in beans, salt, sugar, and shortening. Gradually add 4 cups flour, stirring with spoon as flour is added. Add enough of remaining flour to handle easily. Knead until smooth and elastic. • Place in greased bowl and grease top. Cover and let rise until doubled (about 1 hour). Punch down and let rise again. • Divide dough into 2 loaves. Cover and let rise in pans. Bake at 350 degrees for 50 minutes.

Makes two loaves.

Pinto Bean Muffins

I cup cooked, mashed pinto beans
2 eggs
I cup milk
4 Tbsp. shortening, melted
I tsp. salt
2 tsp. brown sugar
2 cups flour
2 tsp. baking powder

Mix dry ingredients. In separate bowl, beat eggs. Mix with milk and mashed beans. Add melted shortening and mix just enough to moisten dry ingredients. • Fill muffin tins half full and bake at 400 degrees for 20–30 minutes. Serve hot with butter.

Pinto Bean Pie

2 eggs, well beaten
1 cup sugar
1 cup cooked, mashed pinto beans
1 cup evaporated milk
½ cup coconut
2 tsp. vanilla
⅛ tsp. salt

Mix all ingredients together well and pour into a pie dish lined with pie crust (pg. 40). • Bake at 350 degrees for 45 minutes. When cool, top with Dream Whip (pg. 43).

Bean Chowder

¾ cup dry beans
1 Tbsp. margarine
¾ cup chopped green peppers
3 cups water
1½ tsp. salt
1½ cups milk
½ cup chopped onion
1½ tsp. flour
¾ cup diced potatoes
¾ cup tomatoes

Soak the beans overnight. Add salt and boil. Cover with a lid until almost softened, about 1 hour. Add potato and onion. Cook 30 minutes more. • Mix flour and margarine, and stir into the beans. Add the tomatoes and green pepper. • Cook over low heat about 10 minutes until thickened. Stir in the milk and serve.

Ham Hock Soup

about 7 cups water
1 ham hock
salt and pepper to taste
¾ cup soup mix

Simmer all ingredients for 45 minutes or until tender. Remove ham hock. Trim off meat and return meat to soup.

Makes 6 servings.

 ## Using Dried Carrots

• Carrots are a great addition to your food storage. They add vitamin A to meals and make your soups and stews more substantial.

• But be careful not to overdo it. These carrots will at least double in size when reconstituted. So, if in doubt, reconstitute before adding them into things.

• To reconstitute, just cover the carrots with a little over twice the amount of boiling water as carrots. (It doesn't matter if you use too much water because you are going to drain them anyway.) Let stand for 20–25 minutes. Drain and measure what you want. You can just toss them dry into all kinds of soups, just a half of handful or so. They come in handy when you don't have fresh carrots around.

Scrumptious Carrot Cake

3-4 cups boiling water
2 tsp. baking soda
1½ cups dried carrots
2 tsp. cinnamon
2 cups flour
4 eggs
1½ cups vegetable oil
½ tsp. nutmeg
1 cup brown sugar
1 cup sugar
2 tsp. baking powder
1 cup chopped nuts
1 tsp. salt

Pour boiling water over dried carrots. Let stand about 20–25 minutes to reconstitute. Drain and measure 3 cups of the reconstituted carrots. • Grease and flour 2 (9-inch) round cake pans or 1 (9x13-inch) pan. • In a large bowl, combine dry ingredients. • In a small bowl, beat eggs and oil. Add to dry mixture. Mix until well blended. Fold in carrots and chopped nuts. • Pour into prepared baking pans. Bake 25–30 minutes or until toothpick comes out clean. Cool in pans on rack 10 minutes. Turn out onto a rack to cool completely. When cool, frost with Cream Cheese Frosting (pg. 90).

Cream Cheese Frosting

1 (8-oz.) pkg. cream cheese, softened, or Cream Cheese
    Yogurt (pg. 106)
2 tsp. vanilla
½ cup butter, softened
1 lb. powdered sugar
1 cup chopped nuts (optional)

In a medium bowl, beat cream cheese and butter until
fluffy. Blend in vanilla. Gradually add powdered sugar. Beat
until smooth and creamy. Fold in chopped nuts, if desired,
reserving 2 Tbsp. to garnish the top of the cake. Spread
frosting over sides and top of cake.

Carrot Cookies

¾ cup sugar
2 cups flour
¾ cup shortening
1 egg
1 tsp. baking powder
½ tsp. salt
½ cup dried carrots
1 tsp. vanilla
½–1 cup nuts

Pour boiling water over dried carrots. Let stand 20–25
minutes. • Drain carrots, put into a blender along with
the egg, and beat until nearly smooth. Mix remaining
ingredients together and then add carrot-egg mixture along
with the nuts. Mix well. • Spoon dough by teaspoons onto a
greased cookie sheet. Bake at 350 degrees for 15 minutes.

Using Dried Onions

These are great! Use them in any recipe calling for fresh onions. Boost the flavor of your favorite dips, pasta, sauces, soups, and casseroles. Sprinkle over breads, rolls, pizza dough, and biscuits before baking. The sky is the limit! 1 Tbsp. dry onions = 1 small onion. They can be rehydrated before use by soaking in water for 5–10 minutes.

Basic Potato Pearls
• •

2 cups very hot water
1 cup potato pearls

Put potatoes into bowl. Pour water over and stir. They set up quickly.

Makes 4 servings.

Potato Casserole
• •

This simple casserole freezes well, and it's a good side dish for meat that has its own gravy.

2 cups very hot water
¼ cup sour cream, room temperature, or Sour Cream Yogurt
   (pg. 106)
2 oz. cream cheese, room temperature or Cream Cheese Yogurt
   (pg. 106)
salt and pepper to taste
1 cup potato pearls
¼ tsp. onion salt
1 cup shredded cheese (optional)

Prepare potatoes. Add other ingredients. Blend well. • Put into casserole and heat through. Top with shredded cheese if desired.

Potato Soup

2 cups milk or half-and-half
2 cups very hot water
½ cup chicken broth
½ cup finely chopped celery
1 cup potato pearls
½ tsp. onion salt
dash of garlic salt
chopped onion (fresh or dried) to taste

Any or all of the following:
frozen or freeze-dried vegetables
cheese, shredded or powdered
cooked potato cubes
chopped ham
clams

Make potatoes as directed in basic recipe. Stir in the other ingredients. Add chosen options. Heat and serve.

Makes 3–4 servings.

One-Dish Chicken & Rice Bake

1 can cream of mushroom soup
1 cup water
¾ cup uncooked rice
¼ tsp. pepper
¼ tsp. paprika
4 skinless, boneless, chicken breasts

In a 2-quart shallow baking dish, mix soup, water, rice, and seasonings. Lay the chicken breasts out evenly on top.
• Cover and bake at 375 degrees for 1 hour or until chicken in cooked through.

Hot Dog Casserole

1 cup potato pearls
2 cups very hot water
2 tsp. prepared mustard
¼ cup sweet pickle relish
1 Tbsp. minced onion
2 Tbsp. Miracle Whip or mayonnaise
4-6 hot dogs
½ cup shredded cheese

Heat oven to 350 degrees. Prepare potatoes as directed. Stir in relish, Miracle Whip, onion, and mustard. Pour into 1-quart ungreased casserole. • Cut each hot dog in half lengthwise, then in half again crosswise. Put each piece of frank around the edge of the potatoes, standing them up by pushing each one into the edge of the potatoes. • Bake 25–30 minutes, until center is hot. If desired, top with cheese 5 minutes before removing from oven.

Great Little Chicken Recipe

1 (8-oz.) bottle of Russian salad dressing
1 (8-oz.) bottle of apricot preserves
1 (1-oz.) can of tomato sauce
1 envelope of Lipton Onion Soup Mix
4-6 boneless, skinless, chicken breasts or chicken pieces

Mix dressing, preserves, tomato sauce, and soup mix. Pour over chicken and cover. • Bake at 350 degrees for 1 hour. Serve with rice.

Hamburger Pie

1 lb. ground beef
½ onion, chopped
1 (16-oz.) can cut green beans
1 can tomato soup
pinch of thyme
pinch of marjoram
dash of chili powder
1 beaten egg
dash of oregano
½ cup shredded cheese
3 cups water, very hot
1½ cups potato pearls

Prepare potatoes using 1½ cup potato pearls and 3 cups very hot water. Set aside. • In a large skillet, cook ground beef and onion until meat is browned and onion is tender. Drain off fat. Stir in beans, soup, ¼ cup water, ¾ tsp. salt, and ⅛ tsp. pepper. • Turn mixture into a 1½-quart casserole dish. Stir egg into the mashed potatoes. Season with salt and pepper. • Drop potatoes in mounds on top of meat mixture. Sprinkle with cheese. • Bake uncovered at 350 degrees for 25–30 minutes or until heated thoroughly.

Makes 4–6 servings.

Never-Fail Whole Wheat Bread

8½ cups warm water (105–115 degrees)
1 cup potato pearls
½ cup honey
1 cup non-instant powdered milk
6 Tbsp. yeast
3 Tbsp. salt
½ cup vegetable oil
22 cups whole wheat flour

Sprinkle yeast on water; add honey and oil. Let stand about 5 minutes until bubbly. Add potato pearls, powdered milk, salt, and about 10 cups flour. Mix using electric mixer (or bread dough hook) for 5 minutes. Let dough stand for about 15 minutes. • Add remaining flour and knead (by hand or mixer) about 5 minutes more. • Divide dough and form into 6 loaves. Using non-stick spray, grease 6 (8½x4½-inch) loaf pans. Place loaves in pans and let rise until doubled in size. • Bake 20 minutes at 350 degrees and 20 more minutes at 325 degrees, depending on the oven. Immediately turn out onto rack to cool after baking. • Brush tops with butter or cover loosely with foil to keep crust from getting hard.

Makes 6 loaves.

Chicken Rice Casserole

3 cups cooked rice
1 cup sour cream
1 can cream of chicken soup
1 cup shredded cheddar cheese
2 cups cooked, cut up chicken
1 (16-oz.) pkg. frozen broccoli, cooked
¼ cup melted butter
2 cups corn flakes, crushed

Spread the rice evenly on the bottom of a greased 9x13-inch baking dish. Evenly spread out the broccoli and chicken chunks over the rice. Combine the soup and sour cream and spread this evenly over the casserole. Mix cornflakes and melted butter; spread over the top. • Bake at 350 degrees for 30–40 minutes.

Variation
• Instead of rice you can use diced or sliced potatoes.

 ## Using Dried Apples

You can rehydrate dried apples for all of your favorite apple recipes. If the recipe calls for 4 cups of apples, put 2 cups of dried apples into a large container. Boil 4 scant cups of water and pour over the apples; let stand for 45 minutes. **Do not drain!** They are ready to use in your favorite recipes. If you put this mixture through the blender, you will have applesauce.

Grandma's Apple Dessert
• •

This is good enough to double!

2 cups sliced apples
1 tsp. flour
1 tsp. cinnamon
1 dash of salt
½ cup flour
½ cup rolled oats
½ cup brown sugar
¼ cup butter

Mix apples, flour, cinnamon, and salt, and place in a 9-inch baking dish. • In separate bowl, mix remaining dry ingredients. Cut in butter and mix until crumbly. Sprinkle over apples. • Bake at 350 degrees 30–40 minutes until apples are tender and top is lightly browned.

Apple Pie
• •

1⅔ cups dried apple slices
2½ cups water
⅔ cup sugar
2 Tbsp. cornstarch
¼ tsp. salt
1 tsp. cinnamon
½ tsp. nutmeg
3 Tbsp. lemon juice

Prepare pie crust (p. 40, 60). Put all ingredients in a saucepan and bring to a boil. Boil for 1 minute, stirring so that it will not burn. Pour into pastry shell and cover with top pastry. • Flute edges and bake at 425 degrees for 35–40 minutes or until lightly browned.

Dutch Apple Pie

2 cups dried apples, firmly packed
2 cups boiling water
⅓ cup sugar
2 Tbsp. flour
½ tsp. cinnamon

Prepare pie crust (pg. 40, 60). In medium saucepan, pour boiling water over apples, and let set for at least 5 minutes. • In separate bowl, mix sugar, flour, and cinnamon. Add to the apples and cook over medium heat until thick. Stir constantly to prevent scorching. • Pour mixture into unbaked pie shell and dot with butter.

Topping:
⅓ cup brown sugar
½ cup flour
¼ cup butter

Cut in butter until crumbly. Sprinkle over the apple mixture and bake in a 350-degree oven for 55 minutes.

Apple Syrup

¾ cup water
1½ cups sugar
1 Tbsp. corn syrup
4 Tbsp. apple juice concentrate
2 Tbsp. cornstarch

Combine first 3 ingredients in a saucepan and bring to a boil. Stir until sugar is dissolved. Combine apple juice concentrate with cornstarch. Add to saucepan. • Cook and stir until it is clear.

Apple Nut Dessert

1 cup sugar
2 tsp. baking powder
¾ cup flour
1 Tbsp. shortening
½ cup evaporated milk
1 tsp. vanilla
½ cup chopped nuts
3 cups chopped, peeled apples

Mix sugar, baking powder, flour, and shortening. Stir in milk and vanilla. Add nuts and apples. • Spread in 9-inch square pan.

Topping:
2 Tbsp. brown sugar
2 Tbsp. margarine
⅓ cup flour

Combine sugar and flour. Cut in butter until crumbly. Sprinkle over the apple mixture. Bake at 400 degrees for 30–35 minutes.

Apple Brown Betty

2 cups boiling water
4 cups dried apples
¼ cup butter

Topping:
½ cup flour
¼ cup oatmeal
½ tsp. cinnamon
¼ cup brown sugar

Pour boiling water over apples. Let stand at least 5 minutes. Combine well and then cut in butter. Place apples with the remaining liquid in a greased 9x9-inch pan. Sprinkle topping over the apples. • Bake at 350 degrees for 55 minutes.

Apple Crisp

4 cups apple slices
8 cups water
½ cup sugar
2 tsp. cinnamon, divided
6 Tbsp. butter or margarine
¾ cup flour
½ cup brown sugar

In large pan, bring apple slices, water, sugar, and 1 tsp. cinnamon to a boil. Reduce heat and simmer for about 30 minutes. Drain off liquid, returning 1 cup of liquid to apple mixture. • In separate bowl, mix brown sugar, flour, butter, and 1 tsp. cinnamon until crumbly. • Preheat oven to 325 degrees. Put fruit in one lightly greased large casserole dish or 2 (9-inch) pie pans. Sprinkle crumb topping over it. Bake uncovered for 1 hour.

Apple Pudding

1 cup sugar
¼ cup butter
3 cups chopped apples
1 cup flour
1 tsp. soda
1 tsp. cinnamon
dash of salt
½ cup chopped nuts

Cream sugar and butter. Add remaining ingredients. Pour into 9x9-inch pan. • Bake in 350 degree oven for 30 minutes. Serve with Cream Sauce (pg. 101).

Cream Sauce

¼ cup butter
1 tsp. vanilla
½ cup brown sugar
½ cup white sugar
½ cup sweet cream

Heat, while stirring, until smooth. Serve warm.

Pumpkin Apple Streusel Muffins

2½ cups all-purpose flour
2 cups sugar
1 Tbsp. pumpkin pie spice
1 tsp. baking soda
2 eggs, lightly beaten
½ tsp. salt
½ cup vegetable oil
1 cup pumpkin
2 cups finely chopped peeled apples

Streusel:
2 Tbsp. all-purpose flour
¼ cup sugar
4 tsp. butter or margarine, softened
½ tsp. cinnamon

In a large bowl, combine flour, sugar, pumpkin pie spice, soda, and salt; set aside. • In another bowl, combine eggs, pumpkin, and oil. Stir pumpkin mixture into dry ingredients just until moistened. Stir in apples. • Spoon batter into greased muffin tins, filling ¾ full. Combine streusel ingredients and sprinkle over batter. • Bake at 400 degrees for 20–22 minutes or until toothpick comes out clean.

Makes 2 dozen muffins.

Applesauce Oatmeal Cookies

1 cup shortening
2 cups sugar
2 cups applesauce
2 eggs
2 tsp. soda
1 tsp. cinnamon
1 tsp. nutmeg
1 tsp. cloves
3½ cups flour
1 tsp. salt
1 cup chopped nuts
2 cups oatmeal
1 cup chocolate chips (optional)
1 cup raisins (optional)

Cream together shortening and sugar. Add eggs and applesauce. Mix well and then add the rest of the ingredients. • Mix well again and drop by spoonful onto greased baking sheet. Bake at 350 degrees for 10–12 minutes.

Apple Chip Cake

2 eggs
2 cups sugar
2 tsp. vanilla
4 cups reconstituted apples
3 cups flour
1 tsp. cinnamon
2 tsp. soda
⅔ cup oil

Beat eggs. Add sugar and vanilla. Add apples. Stir in flour, cinnamon, and soda. Add oil. • Mix well and pour into a 9x13-inch baking pan. Sprinkle batter with Crumb Cake Topping (pg. 103) and bake at 350 degrees for 50–60 minutes.

Crumb Cake Topping

1 cup chopped nuts
½ cup flour
½ cup margarine
1 cup brown sugar

Mix dry ingredients. Cut in margarine until crumbly.

Apple-Filled Cookies

1 cup butter
1¾ cup brown sugar
1 tsp. vanilla
¼ tsp. cinnamon
2 eggs
½ cup water
½ tsp. salt
1 tsp. soda
3½ cups flour (wheat or white)

Blend together all ingredients except flour in large bowl. Blend in flour. • Drop by teaspoons onto an ungreased cookie sheet. Make a depression in the middle of each drop and place small amount of apple filling (recipe below) in the depression. Then put about ½ tsp. of dough on top of filling. • Bake at 350 degrees for about 12 minutes.

Filling:
2 cups dried apples
¾ cup water
½ cup chopped nuts
½ cup sugar
1 Tbsp. flour

Chop apples into small pieces. **Do not reconstitute!** Place in a saucepan and add remaining ingredients. Cook together slowly, stirring constantly to prevent scorching, until thick. Cool.

Apple Harvest Squares

1½ cups flour
½ tsp. salt
½ cup butter or margarine
1 cup sugar, divided
4 cups reconstituted apples
2 Tbsp. lemon juice
1 egg, lightly beaten
1 tsp. cinnamon
⅓ cup evaporated milk
1 tsp. vanilla
1⅓ cups flaked coconut
¾ cup chopped nuts

Combine flour, salt, and ⅓ cup sugar. Cut in butter until the mixture resembles fine crumbs. • Press into the bottom of a greased 9x13-inch pan. Arrange the apples on top of the crumbs and sprinkle with lemon juice. • Combine ⅓ cup sugar with cinnamon. Sprinkle over the apples. • Bake at 375 degrees for 20 minutes. • Meanwhile, in a small bowl, combine remaining sugar with the rest of the ingredients. • Spoon over the apples. Bake for another 20 minutes or until golden brown. Cut into squares while still warm.

Makes about 20 servings.

Cocoa Mix

15 cups instant powdered milk
1 cup cocoa
1½ cups sugar
1½ tsp. salt

Mix well. To use, mix ½ cup mix with 1 cup hot water.

Makes enough for 10 quarts or 40 1-cup servings.

Yogurt

7 cups warm water, divided
2½ cups non-instant powdered milk
6 oz. store-bought yogurt or ½ cup plain homemade yogurt

In a blender, combine 3 cups warm water and milk. Blend on low. Add yogurt and 4 cups warm water. • Pour into jars, put lids on, and place in a pan or bowl of warm water (100–110 degrees). The water should cover most of the jar. • Keep at that temperature for 6–24 hours until set, depending on the freshness of your yogurt start and the temperature. • For best results, the yogurt start that is used should be fresh. If using commercial yogurt, it shouldn't be near the expiration date.

Variations:
Fruit yogurt: Mix yogurt with sweetened fruit preserves and, if you desire, powdered sugar or honey. Can be used in smoothies and frozen treats.

 Keeping your yogurt at temperature

There are quite a few different methods to keep your yogurt at the temperature you want it:

1. Use a heating pad. Place it under the pan with the jars of yogurt and warm water.
2. Use an electric frying pan. Place the pan with jars of yogurt in water in a frying pan, set to approximately 110 degrees.
3. Put the pan with jars of yogurt in a cooler; place outside in the sun on a warm day.
4. Turn on the oven just for a few seconds, enough to warm oven slightly. Turn on oven light. Place pan with water and jars of yogurt as close to the light as possible and let sit overnight.

Sour Cream Yogurt

7 cups warm water, divided
3¾ cups non-instant powdered milk
½ cup plain homemade yogurt, or 6 oz. store-bought yogurt

In a blender, combine 3 cups warm water and milk. Blend on low. Add yogurt and 4 cups warm water. • Pour into jars, put lids on, and place in a pan or bowl of warm water (100–110 degrees). The water should cover most of the jar. • Keep at that temperature for 6–24 hours until set, depending on the freshness of your yogurt start and the temperature.

Cream Cheese Yogurt

7 cups warm water
5 cups non-instant powdered milk
½ cup plain homemade yogurt (or 6 oz. store-bought yogurt)

In a blender, combine 3 cups warm water and milk. Blend on low. Add yogurt and 4 cups warm water. • Pour into jars, put lids on, and place in a pan or bowl of warm water (100–110 degrees). The water should cover most of the jar. • Keep at that temperature for 6–24 hours until set, depending on the freshness of your yogurt start and the temperature.

❓ Can I substitute yogurts for sour cream and cream cheese?

Sour cream yogurt and cream cheese yogurt make excellent substitutions for sour cream and cream cheese in casserole recipes and baked goods. Nutritionally, this improves the recipe by adding, per cup substituted, approximately 330 more mg. of calcium and at least 9 g. more protein than regular sour cream, without adding the 48 g. of fat found in a cup of regular sour cream.

 ## Freezing Yogurts

For quick use, freeze yogurts in convenient recipe-sized portions and just pull one out of the freezer in time to thaw before use.

Day Cheese

4 cups water
1½ cups non-instant powdered milk
½ tsp. salt
2–4 Tbsp. lemon juice or vinegar

Mix water and powdered milk. Place in a pan on low heat. Add slowly a little drizzle of lemon juice or vinegar, and stir gently. If using lemon juice, make sure it hasn't expired. If it is old, it might need to be replaced for this recipe to work. • Continue to gently stir while milk cooks; don't let it come to a boil. Milk will gradually develop curds and separate from the whey, which will be almost clear. If it does not turn into curds and whey, add a little more lemon juice or vinegar. • Strain and rinse the curds in cool water. Add salt.

 ## Cheesecloth care

Cheesecloth is reusable but should be washed in cold water before it is washed in hot soapy water, otherwise, the cheese may melt into the cloth.

Cottage Cheese

¼ rennet tablet
1 quart warm water
3 cups non-instant powdered milk
½ cup buttermilk

In 1 quart warm water, dissolve ¼ of a rennet tablet. (Junket is a brand name of rennet that you can find in most grocery stores in the Jell-O section.) • Combine water, milk, and buttermilk in blender. Blend on low. Add to dissolved rennet-water mixture. Stir well, then let set in warm room 6–12 hours. It is set when it's firm and has a touch of whey on the sides. • When it is set, cut into ½-inch squares and set the bowl in a sink or bigger bowl of hot water. Gently stir the curds at frequent intervals to warm evenly and break up the curds. When they have warmed through and broken into curds and whey, pour through a strainer with a cheesecloth lining. Drain and rinse with cold water until it is cool and well washed. Add salt (around 1 tsp., depending on taste). To make it creamy, you can then add milk and cream.

Parmesan Cheese Sauce

This sauce is great on fish, baked chicken or pork, steamed vegetables, and pasta.

1½ cup chicken broth, divided
2 Tbsp. flour
⅓ cup non-instant powdered milk
½ cup Parmesan cheese

In a large bowl, blend ¾ cup broth, flour, and milk. In small pot, bring remaining ¾ cup of the broth to a boil. Reduce heat and stir blended ingredients into boiling broth. • Bring to a boil, and cook approximately 2 minutes or until sauce thickens. • Remove from heat. Stir in Parmesan cheese.

Bakers' Cheese

Follow recipe for cottage cheese (pg. 108) except after cheese has set, put in a cheesecloth-lined colander and strain out whey until the cheese reaches the consistency of cream cheese. It usually takes all day or all night.

 ## How do I use Bakers' Cheese?

Bakers' Cheese can be substituted for most soft cheeses, especially cream cheese. It makes an excellent substitute for cream cheese in dips and baked goods if you don't want the tartness of the cream cheese yogurt (pg. 106). While 1 cup of cream cheese has 80 g. of fat and 184 mg. of calcium, 1 cup of bakers cheese has less than 1 g. of fat and approximately 400 mg. of calcium. Try freezing it in convenient recipe-sized portions.

Buttermilk

1 cup non-instant powdered milk
3 cups slightly warm water
½ cup commercial or previously made buttermilk

Blend in blender until blended. Cover and allow to stand at room temperature until clabbered (thickened and curdled), about 6–12 hours. Refrigerate after clabbering. Buy commercial buttermilk occasionally for a fresh start.

Makes 1 quart.

Using powdered milk in sauces and soups

The following are just examples of the milk-based sauces and soups that you can make with powdered milk instead of milk, half-and-half, or cream. You can adapt your favorite recipes by blending the powdered milk and other ingredients with some of the liquid (either broth or water) and then adding this mixture to the rest of the liquid in a saucepan when it is boiling. You can modify the thickness of the sauce by adding more or less flour. For creamier sauces add more milk powder.

Allemande Sauce
• •

This versatile sauce is great in chicken dishes such as chicken a la king, chicken cordon bleu, chicken and broccoli casserole, etc.

1 cup chicken broth or bouillon and water, divided
2 Tbsp. flour
¼ tsp. salt
¼ cup non-instant powdered milk
1 egg
3 Tbsp. butter
1 Tbsp. lemon juice

In small pot, bring ½ cup of the broth or water to a boil. • In a separate bowl, blend the remaining broth, flour, salt, milk, and egg. Reduce heat and stir blended ingredients into the boiling broth. Bring to boil. Cook 1 minute, stirring constantly. Stir in butter and lemon juice.

Variations:
Use as a substitute for commercial cream of chicken soup by making the chicken broth slightly more concentrated by adding 1½–2 bouillon cubes per cup of water and adding 1 Tbsp. more of flour.

Corn Chowder

½ lb. bacon
½ cup chopped onion
½ cup chopped celery
4 cups water, divided
2 cups diced or shredded potatoes
¾ cup non-instant milk powder
2 Tbsp. flour
1 tsp. salt
¼ tsp. pepper
1 can cream-style corn or blended whole-kernel corn

Fry bacon until crisp. Remove bacon and discard all but
2 Tbsp. bacon grease. Sauté onion and celery in reserved
bacon grease. Add 3 cups water and potatoes. Simmer until
tender. • Blend 1 cup water, milk powder, flour, salt, and
pepper. Add mixture to pan of simmering potatoes. Add
corn. Heat and sprinkle with reserved bacon.

Basic Smoothies

¼ cup Tang or other fruit drink mix
¼ cup non-instant dry milk
2 Tbsp. sugar
1½ cups water
2 cups ice
fresh or frozen fruit (recommendations: bananas, strawberries,
pineapple, mango, peach)
1 cup yogurt (optional)

Put water in blender. While blending, add the rest of the
ingredients. Blend until smooth.

Basic Pudding & Pie Filling

½ cup sugar
3 Tbsp. flour
1 Tbsp. cornstarch
¼ tsp. salt
⅓ cup non-instant powdered milk
1 egg
1 Tbsp. butter
1¾ cups water (1½ cups for pie filling)
1 tsp. vanilla

Bring half of the water to a boil. Take the other half of the water and blend with the dry ingredients and the egg in a blender; add to the boiling water. • After it comes back to a boil, cook for 1 minute, stirring constantly. Remove from heat; stir in the butter and vanilla.

Variations:
Chocolate flavored: Add 2 Tbsp. of cocoa to the dry ingredients.
Coconut flavored: Add ½ cup shredded coconut. Use coconut flavoring instead of vanilla.
Caramel flavored: Use ½ cup brown sugar instead of white.

Healthy Chip Dip

2 cups cottage cheese
¼–½ cup yogurt (optional)
2-3 Tbsp. of your desired seasonings or dip mixes

Blend cottage cheese until smooth. Add yogurt and seasoning. • If following the directions for a packaged mix, just substitute the same amount of blended cottage cheese for the sour cream. You'll have a much healthier dip with no fat.

Easy Cheesecake

½ cup warm water
¾ cup non-instant powdered milk
¾ cup sugar
¼ cup lemon juice or orange juice
1 tsp. vanilla
1 cup cream cheese or Cream Cheese Yogurt (pg. 106) or Bakers' Cheese (pg. 109)

Put warm water in blender and turn to medium. While running the blender, add all ingredients. Pour mixture quickly into graham cracker crust.

Key Lime Pie

2 cups sweetened condensed milk (pg. 109)
½ cup lime juice
3 egg yolks
1 drop of green food coloring, if desired

With blender or electric beaters, beat ingredients. Pour into graham cracker crust (pg. 38). • Bake 30 minutes at 325 degrees. Chill.

• Part 3 •

Substitutions and Measurements

"As long as I can remember, we have been taught to prepare for the future and to obtain a year's supply of necessities. I would guess that the years of plenty have almost universally caused us to set aside this counsel. I believe the time to disregard this counsel is over. With events in the world today, it must be considered with all seriousness."[3]

• Elder L. Tom Perry

Substitutions

● ●

At times it is necessary to use a substitution for a recipe ingredient. The substituted food may not perform exactly as the original food. Each ingredient has specific functions in a recipe, and a substitute may alter the flavor, color, texture, or volume, but still results in an acceptable finished product.[4]

Ingredient	Amount	Substitutions
Allspice	1 tsp.	½ tsp. cinnamon and ½ tsp. ground cloves
Apple pie spice	1 tsp.	½ tsp. cinnamon, ¼ tsp. nutmeg, and ⅛ tsp. cardamom
Baking powder	1 tsp.	¼ tsp. baking soda and ⅝ tsp. cream of tartar, **or** ¼ tsp. baking soda and ½ cup soured milk or buttermilk, **or** ¼ tsp. baking soda and ½ Tbsp. vinegar or lemon juice with enough whole milk to make ½ cup, **or** ¼ tsp. baking soda and ¼–½ tsp. molasses
Butter	1 cup	1 cup margarine, **or** ⅞ cup lard and ½ tsp. salt, **or** ⅘ cups bacon fat, clarified, **or** ⅞ cup oil
Buttermilk or sour milk	1 cup	1 Tbsp. vinegar or lemon juice and enough whole milk to make 1 cup (let stand 5 minutes), **or** 1¾ tsp. cream of tartar and 1 cup whole milk, **or** 1 cup plain yogurt
Chocolate, baking	1 oz.	3 Tbsp. cocoa and 1 Tbsp. fat
Chocolate, semisweet	1 oz.	½ oz. baking chocolate and 1 Tbsp. sugar
Cornmeal, self-rising	1 cup	⅞ cup plain cornmeal, 1½ Tbsp. baking powder, and ½ tsp. salt

Cornstarch	1 Tbsp.	1 Tbsp. all-purpose flour, **or** 2 Tbsp. granular tapioca
Corn syrup	1 cup	1 cup sugar and ¼ cup liquid
Corn syrup, dark	1 cup	¾ cup light corn syrup and ¼ cup molasses
Cream, half & half (12–16% fat)	1 cup	⅞ cup milk and 1½ Tbsp. butter (for use in cooking), **or** 1 cup evaporated milk, undiluted
Cream, light (18–20% fat)	1 cup	⅞ cup milk and 3 Tbsp. butter or margarine (for use in cooking or baking), **or** 1 cup evaporated milk, undiluted
Cream, heavy (36–40% fat)	1 cup (2½ cups whipped)	¾ cup milk and ⅓ cup butter/margarine (for use in cooking or baking)
Cocoa	¼ cup	1 oz. unsweetened chocolate (decrease fat called for in recipe by ½ Tbsp.)
Egg, whole	1 large	2 egg yolks, **or** 1 tsp. unflavored gelatin, 3 Tbsp. cold water, and 2 Tbsp. plus 1 tsp. boiling water (for use in baking), **or** 2 Tbsp. plus 2 tsp. dry whole egg powder and an equal amount water
Egg yolk	1½ Tbsp.	3½ tsp. thawed frozen egg, **or** 2 tsp. dry egg yolk and 2 tsp. water
Egg white	2 Tbsp.	2 tsp. dry whites and 2 Tbsp. water
Flour, as thickener	1 Tbsp.	½ Tbsp. cornstarch, potato starch, rice starch, or arrowroot starch, **or** 1 Tbsp. quick-cooking tapioca
Flour, all-purpose	1 cup, sifted	1 cup all-purpose flour minus 2 Tbsp. **or** 1 cup plus 2 Tbsp. cake flour
Flour, cake	1 cup, sifted	1 cup minus 2 Tbsp. sifted all-purpose flour

Flour, self-rising	1 cup, sifted	1 cup all-purpose flour, 1½ tsp. baking powder, and ½ tsp. salt
Flour, whole wheat	1 cup	1 cup all-purpose flour
Gelatin, flavored	3 oz.	1 Tbsp. plain gelatin and 2 cups fruit juice
Honey	1 cup	1¼ cups sugar and ¼ cup liquid
Lemon	3 oz. or 1 medium	1–3 Tbsp. juice and 1–2 tsp. grated peel
Lemon juice	1 tsp.	½ tsp. vinegar
Milk	1 cup	⅓ cup instant nonfat powdered milk and ½ cup minus 1 Tbsp. water, **or** 3 Tbsp. sifted regular nonfat powdered milk and 1 cup minus 1 Tbsp. water
Milk, sweetened condensed	1⅓ cup or 1 can	1 cup plus 2 Tbsp. powdered milk and ½ cup warm water; mix well, add ¾ cup sugar and 3 Tbsp. melted butter/margarine
Milk, whole	1 cup	⅓ cup instant nonfat powdered milk and 2½ tsp. butter/margarine, **or** ½ cup evaporated milk and ½ cup water, **or** ¼ cup sifted dry whole milk powder and ⅞ cup water
Oil*	1 cup	1 melted shortening
Pumpkin pie spice	1 tsp.	½ tsp. cinnamon, ¼ tsp. ginger, ⅛ tsp. allspice, ⅛ tsp. nutmeg
Shortening, solid	1 cup	⅞ cup lard, **or** 1⅛ cup butter/margarine (decrease salt in recipe by ½)
Shortening, melted	1 cup	1 cup oil
Sour cream	1 cup	1 cup plain yogurt, **or** ⅞ cup sour milk and ⅓ cup butter

Sugar, dark brown	1 cup	1 cup granulated sugar
Sugar, light brown	1 cup	½ cup dark brown sugar and ½ cup granulated sugar
Sugar, granulated	1 cup	1 cup corn syrup (decrease liquid called for in recipe by ¼ cup), **or** 1 cup molasses (decrease liquid called for in recipe by ¼ cup), **or** ¾ cup honey (decrease liquid called for in recipe by ¼ cup; for each cup of honey in baked goods, add ½ tsp. soda)
Yeast, active dry	1 Tbsp.	1 compressed yeast cake

* Do not substitute oil for solid fat in a baking recipe. Characteristics of the final product could be significantly different.

Equivalent Measures

1 gallon	4 quarts
1 quart	2 pints
1 pint	2 cups
1 bushel	4 pecks
1 peck	8 quarts
1 cup	16 Tbsp.
⅞ cup	14 Tbsp. or 1 cup minus 2 Tbsp.
¾ cup	12 Tbsp.
⅔ cup	10⅔ Tbsp.
⅝ cup	10 Tbsp.
½ cup	8 Tbsp.
⅓ cup	5⅓ Tbsp.
¼ cup	4 Tbsp.
⅛ cup	2 Tbsp.
¹⁄₁₆ cup	1 Tbsp.
1 Tbsp.	3 tsp.
¾ Tbsp.	2¼ tsp.
⅔ Tbsp.	2 tsp.
½ Tbsp.	1½ tsp.
⅓ Tbsp.	1 tsp.
¼ Tbsp.	¾ tsp.
pinch or dash	¹⁄₁₆ tsp.

Part 4

Shelf Life

"In reviewing the Lord's counsel to us on the importance of preparedness, I am impressed with the plainness of the message. The Savior made it clear that we cannot place sufficient oil in our preparedness lamps by simply avoiding evil. We must also be anxiously engaged in a positive program of preparation."[5]

· Elder L. Tom Perry

Shelf Life
("Best if used by" Recommendations)

Product	Shelf Life
Sugar	20+ years
Wheat	20+ years
Carrots	10 years
Fruit drink mix	10 years
Beans, dry pinto	8 years
Beans, dry pink	8 years
Beans, dry white	8 years
Apple slices	8 years
Spaghetti	8 years
Macaroni	8 years
Chopped dry onions	8 years
Hot cocoa	5 years
Rolled oats	5 years
Vanilla pudding	5 years
Chocolate pudding	5 years
White flour	5 years
Soup mix	5 years
Rice	4 years
Nonfat powdered milk	3 years
Potato pearls	3 years

 Storage suggestions

Store dry-pack items in a cool, dry location (70 degrees or cooler) away from sunlight. Store on shelves or on raised platforms rather than directly in contact with concrete floors or walls. Rotation can be accomplished by personal use or by sharing with others.

Are there things that shouldn't be canned?

Some products do not store well in cans because of moisture, oil, or other concerns. These products and emergency supplies such as first-aid kits and food rations (candy, granola bars, etc.) are best stored when rotated frequently:

Baking powder
Baking soda
Bouillon
Brown rice
Brown sugar
Chewy dehydrated fruit
Cornmeal
Dried eggs
Dried meat
Granola
Mixes containing leavening (such as pancake or
     biscuit mix)
Nuts (roasted or raw)
Oil
Pearled barley
Raisins
Salt
Spices
Whole wheat flour
Yeast

Works Cited

1. Gordon B. Hinckley, "To Men of the Priesthood," *Ensign*, Nov. 2002, 58.
2. Random Sampler, "Update on Milk Storage," *Ensign*, Mar. 1997, 70–71.
3. L. Tom Perry, "If Ye Are Prepared Ye Shall Not Fear," *Ensign*, Nov. 1995, 36.
4. American Home Economics Association, *Handbook of Food Preparation*, 8th ed., Dudbuque, IA, 1993.
   "Ingredient Substitution and Equivalent Chart," Circular HE-585. Oleane Carden Zenoble, Alabama Cooperative Extension Service, Auburn University.
5. L. Tom Perry, "If Ye Are Prepared Ye Shall Not Fear," *Ensign*, Nov. 1995, 36.

Index